CLOTHED IN CHRIST

CLOTHED IN CHRIST

The Sacraments and Christian Living

Michael Downey

CROSSROAD • NEW YORK

1987

The Crossroad Publishing Company
370 Lexington Avenue, New York, N.Y. 10017

Printed in the United States of America

Library of Congress Cataloging in Publication Data

Downey, Michael.
  Clothed in Christ.

  Includes index.
  1. Sacraments—Catholic Church.   2. Christian life—
Catholic authors.   3. Christian ethics—Catholic authors.
4. Catholic Church—Doctrines.   I. Title.
BX2200.D58 1987   234'.16   87-13428
ISBN 0-8245-0812-2

To my mothers and sisters in faith

All baptized in Christ, you have
all clothed yourselves in Christ, and
there are no more distinctions between Jew
and Greek, slave and free, male and female,
but all of you are one in Christ Jesus.

Galatians 3:27–28

CONTENTS

Acknowledgments

The heart's memory is a vast inner space within which the names and faces of many are held. In acknowledging those who have been of assistance in this work, I offer my deepest gratitude to all of those kept in the memory of my heart.

David Power, professor and chair of the Department of Theology at the Catholic University of America, has shown interest and encouragement in this work from its inception.

Paul Philibert, president of the Dominican School of Philosophy and Theology at Berkeley, offered helpful insights from his expertise in moral theology and psychology.

Gerard Austin, associate professor of liturgical studies at the Catholic University of America, introduced me to the study of liturgy and sacraments.

Tiina Allik, colleague and friend, has offered example and consolation by her intellectual honesty, personal integrity and commitment to the truth. I shall always be grateful for the opportunity to have been her colleague these past five years.

Thomas P. Rausch, ecumenist and professor of theology at Loyola Marymount University, has constantly challenged and critiqued my theological endeavors. He has offered encouragement and support.

Dolores Steinberg, Poor Clare Sister, has provided assistance during this and other writing projects. In acknowledging her generous efforts, I also express my thanks to the sisters of her community.

Irma Pazmiño typed the manuscript in an earlier form. She did so with commitment and care.

Trisha Crissman brought the work to light through its later stages. This she accomplished with a combination of remarkable efficiency and gracious, personal dedication.

Frank Oveis, my editor at Crossroad, has been steadfastly supportive throughout. His magisterial editorial skills together with his prudent exercise of patience, probing, and pressure are deeply appreciated.

For the fiercely loyal friendship of Bob Hurd, and the grace of standing in solidarity with him and Pia Moriarity, his wife, I am thankful beyond the telling of it.

Michael Edward Downey

Introduction

This book is addressed to those who seek to integrate what happens in church and what happens in home, family, work, and political life. It is even concerned with the question of how the sacraments bear upon human relationships of the most intimate kind, and how human intimacy, inclusive of the sexual, is expressed sacramentally. The purpose is to express a sacramental world view that ordinary Catholics might share. This is a vision which views grace as God's presence and self-gift loose in the world. All activity, even the most mundane, is, at least potentially, sacramental activity.

This is not meant to be primarily a practical kind of book. Some readers may be frustrated because their experience of the sacraments and Christian living may not correspond to the vision of sacraments and Christian living which is suggested here.

What is found in these pages is not so much an exposition of the way things actually are, as a vision of *what might be*. Further, the vision is shaped by a conviction about *what can be* based upon the spirit and letter of the Second Vatican Council as well as by the historical development of the sacramental life of the church.

The central thesis of this book is one which derives from the nature of the church as a sacrament in and to the world. Taking the sacramental nature of the church to heart, the aim of this book is to demonstrate that the sacraments themselves express a Christian morality. Some approaches to Christian morality look at Scripture as the guiding norm for the way in which Christians judge, decide, and act. Other approaches might look to the normativity of official church teaching, to natural law theory, or conscience in a focal way. The approach which is taken in this work differs from these others insofar as the guiding conviction throughout is that the contours of the kingdom, the reign of God, which expresses God's intention for the world both now and to come, are to be discerned primarily in and through the sacramental life of the church.

1

Sacraments and Christian Living: A Reciprocal Relationship

There is an intrinsic connection between sacramental celebration and Christian living. How can we more effectively express this connection in our worship and in our daily living? Because of our human limitations and failures, this connection is not always apparent in the lives of those of us who understand ourselves, and are understood by others, as Catholics. Sacraments are often relegated to the "sacred sphere," the church building, and to specific times of the week—Sunday morning for Mass or baptism, Saturday afternoon for marriages. The rest of the week, unless interrupted by a funeral, is taken up with "worldly," or secular, affairs.

The Second Vatican Council has described for us the central contours of the connection between sacraments and Christian living which will be our guide throughout these pages.

Beginnings: The Second Vatican Council

For some Roman Catholics, Vatican II (1962–65) is a fading memory. Those who do remember the days of the council may recall the controversy surrounding some of the changes in church life which originated as a result of this gathering of church leaders. During those years, and for some time thereafter, some were startled by surface changes, like modifications in the traditional dress of religious women; some by more significant changes in the celebration of Mass, like the use of the vernacular and the new position of the altar. Others were amazed to hear of ideas such as the universal call to holiness which was spelled out in the documents issued by the council.[1] The council placed before all baptized Roman Catholics,

1

not just priests and religious, the challenge and responsibility for fully living the Christian life.

More than twenty years later, Catholics are still wrestling with the results of the council. Some look upon it as a historical mistake, and hope somehow it will go away—so that we may return to a type of church life prevalent prior to Vatican II. On the other hand, for many, it is a matter of renewal and reform: the council is looked upon as *the* orienting event of contemporary church life and theology. All Catholic life, teaching, and worship must be shaped by its spirit. By recovering a vision of the church as the People of God, which is based upon an understanding of the church in the New Testament period,[2] the council has recast our understanding of church and Christian living so that it is closer to the gospel and more in keeping with the way people in the second half of the twentieth century actually view the world, and live their lives. Those who view the council as orienting event do not look to a bygone era in the hope that the church may be restored to an imagined pristine past, a pristine past which never in fact existed.[3] Rather, their focus is on the future, on the church as the People of God which is both servant of and witness to the coming of the reign, or kingdom of God.[4] Central to the preaching of Jesus, the reign of God is what God intends for the world both now and to come. Where mercy, justice, truth, unity, and reconciliation are found, the reign of God is near. In brief, the council attempted to raise and give partial answer to the crucial question: What does it mean to be Catholic in the second half of the twentieth century?

The question is crucial if we are willing to recognize that people and societies change over time. The church also changes. People in the twentieth century are quite different than those in the thirteenth. Societal structures are not as they once were. Families and communities in our own time face unique problems and challenges. Change is a fact; whether for better or worse is another and different question.

Those gathered at the council recognized this and set about renewing church life and structures so that they might better answer the urgent demands of our age.

One of the first items on the agenda was the renewal of the sacramental and liturgical life of the church. If the church was to be renewed so as to meet the pressing needs and urgent demands of the contemporary age, it was seen as necessary, first of all, to renew that which is at the heart of Christian life.

It is clear from this that some of those gathered at the Council envisioned a reciprocal relationship between the sacraments and

Christian living. Just as the sacraments influence and shape Christian living, or at least should, so too does Christian living shape sacramental celebration, or at least should. While most Catholics would agree that sacraments should influence their actual Christian lives, they do not know that their experience can be brought to bear upon the form which sacramental celebration takes. This connection was touched upon in the Second Vatican Council's *Constitution on the Sacred Liturgy*. In this document the liturgy is spoken of as "fountain" and "summit" of Christian life (no. 10). The liturgy, or sacramental worship, of the church expresses the fullness of Christ's mystery. But it is that mystery which is to be lived in everyday life, and it is that mystery which leads one to worship in word and sacrament. Christ who is present in sacrament in the reality of his death and Resurrection is the one from whom all grace flows and to whom all creation returns. The Eucharist, from this point of view, is the ritual center of the church's whole sacramental and liturgical system. All other sacraments derive their meaning from their relationship to the Eucharist and have their purpose in drawing Christians more fully into its celebration. From this it follows that there is an intrinsic connection between the way Christians worship and the way they live their lives. Christian living is putting into practice the consequences of belief and sacramental celebration. The concern throughout this book is to show the reciprocal relationship between liturgy and morality, or sacraments and Christian living, by showing that the sacraments themselves express a Christian view of life, and that the way one lives the Christian mystery has bearing upon sacramental celebration of Christ's mysteries.

New Testament Basis

The reciprocal relationship between sacraments and morality, so central to the understanding of those at the council, was also a crucial concern during the New Testament period. In Romans 6 and in Ephesians 5 Paul describes the practical implications of life in Christ for those who are baptized into the Body of Christ, the church.

Romans 6 presents an understanding of baptism with particular attention to the death of Christ. Those who are baptized in Christ Jesus are incorporated into his death. Indeed they enter into the tomb with the dead Christ. United with Christ in his death, the baptized are likewise united in the promise of his Resurrection. This entails a call and a commitment to a new way of living; Ephesians 5 spells out the practical implications of this with respect to a particular way of life—that of marriage in the Lord.

In 1 Corinthians 11 Paul instructs the community that their separate groupings, divisive factions, small-mindedness, and discrimination against persons prevent them from recognizing the Body of Christ in the breaking of the bread and the sharing of the cup, the Eucharist. Those who eat and drink in the name and memory of the Lord, and do not recognize that such separations, factions, and discrimination are opposed to him in whose memory they gather and pray, bring about their own condemnation.

As in the New Testament period, the task for the church now is one of ongoing conversion in Christ, so that what is celebrated in sacrament may be lived out by the Christian community in sight of the world. The community is central to both sacramental celebration and Christian living. They are not primarily individual or private affairs. Precisely those actions which prevent the growth and well-being of the community are condemned by Paul, and cause him to question the value and authenticity of their worship.

With its emphasis upon the church as the People of God, the Second Vatican Council likewise provided the framework for a renewed approach to both sacraments and Christian life which envisions both as rooted in the community of faith. The church is first and foremost the People of God, a community of faith in Christ and confidence in the empowerment of the Spirit. Whatever is said of the sacraments must be said in this light. The community's struggle to live out the liberating message of Jesus in the church and in the world, and its corporate witness to the redemptive value of the cross of Jesus Christ and to the power of his Resurrection provide the basis for understanding sacramental celebration and Christian living.

The Changing Face of Worship

Because of the renewed understanding of the church as the People of God, the community of faith in Jesus Christ and in his Spirit, sacramental life has taken a different shape than the form of worship prior to Vatican II. The history of liturgy and sacramental life is quite varied. Each epoch has worshiped differently, in a manner more or less in keeping with the church's understanding of itself at a given period. In the thirteenth century, for example, the world—indeed the universe—was understood primarily as a rigid hierarchy of being: each and every thing was assigned its proper place and rank in the world order. The notion of a three-storied universe envisioned earth as a kind of midpoint between heaven "up there" and hell "down below." The value of beings rose on an ascending scale.

The visual imagery of higher and lower may tend to misrepresent the real benefits of the hierarchical world view of the thirteenth century. It developed in relation to a valuable philosophical view which, though it may not appeal to contemporary ways of understanding things, is admirable in its own right, and must be respected on its own terms. This view affirms that God is superior in the order of being, that higher realities influence lower realities, and that the more perfect in nature influence the less perfect. Persons, communities, and societies were understood to reflect, as well as participate in, this hierarchical order. The church was viewed as the perfect society on earth precisely because in its own visible hierarchy it mirrored the proper ordering of things, from highest to lowest. This hierarchical ordering was understood to be ordained by God.

The sacramental life of the church during the thirteenth century, and for many centuries following, expressed and fostered this twin understanding of world as hierarchically ordered and of the church as perfect image of that divinely ordained ordering. The central focus in sacramental life was the priest, whose role was to mediate between the higher realm (heavenly or sacred) and the lower realm (earthly or temporal). The priest mediator, because of ordination, was incorporated in a unique way into the perfect, heavenly society here on earth and given power and authority to mediate between the two realms.

Whatever can rightly be argued about the advantages of this thirteenth-century view of church and world, in the realm of sacramental life the consequences of this understanding were for the most part negative. This view of church and world, so forcefully expressed in liturgy and sacrament, reduced the majority of Catholics to the position of observer whose role was to "assist" at Mass, to passively receive the priestly ministration of the mediator between God and humanity.

In our own day the traces of this view of world and church are still to be found. But this understanding was set aside in favor of retrieving the biblical understanding of the church as People of God. No longer is the church envisioned primarily as a hierarchy, but as a community of persons baptized in grace and Spirit. It was also set aside in favor of a renewed understanding of the mission of the church in the world, developed in the council's *Pastoral Constitution on the Church in the Modern World* (nos. 40–45). It is clearer now than before that the church views itself in a relationship of mutuality and critical cooperation with the rest of the world. As a result, the opposition between eternal and temporal, heavenly and earthly, sacred and profane, is overcome to some degree. The church is not only a sign to or for the world but also *in* the world. This is a major change in outlook.

With this understanding of the church, what is expressed in sacramental life today is different from what was expressed in that of the thirteenth-century church. Because it is the community of the baptized which is of primary importance in any sacramental celebration, more attention has been given to the manifold ways in which Christ is present in sacramental celebration: in the People of God who assemble for worship, in the proclamation and hearing of the word, in the various ministers to the community, as well as in the central sacramental activities of the church such as the breaking of bread and sharing of wine, the pouring of the waters of baptism, and the anointing of the sick with blessed oil. Sacramental celebration is understood to be the act of a community of faith, not the action of one of its members done for all the rest. The central role of the community gives rise to greater participation in sacramental life. The Mass is no longer conducted in a language unfamiliar to those assembled for worship, but is celebrated in their own tongue. Responses to the various parts of the liturgy are in themselves acts of participation. The use of liturgical music more in keeping with the cultural experience of a people is likewise an indication of the participatory and communal nature of the church's sacramental life. The altar looks a little less like a shrine and more like a table around which a community gathers to break bread and share the cup. And in the various ministries, which are more and more visible, the church gives expression to the understanding of itself as the People of God.

In its worship and in its life the church is a corporate witness and sign in the world. Like Paul, our attention needs to turn to the ways in which, both in sacrament and in Christian living, we are untrue to the name we bear, thus eating and drinking our own condemnation (1 Cor. 11:17–34). The task is one of daily conversion in Christ so that what we celebrate may be lived out by the Christian community.

On the other side of the coin, however, the community's call to commitment and to conversion demands that what we are living be expressed in worship. That is to say, if we are called to ongoing conversion in Christ so as to live more fully in grace and Spirit, then sacramental celebration itself is part and parcel of that and must itself undergo conversion or change.

We must ask a few hard questions at this point. Does contemporary sacramental celebration "speak" to people in terms of what they are really living, and how they actually view things? Further, is it possible for persons to "speak" in the context of worship and sacrament what they are living, and how they view the world? Or do most of us tend to leave our true selves at home when we put on our Sunday selves and go to Mass? Does the liturgy itself express and impress a vision of God, church, and humanity which is more in keeping with the thirteenth-century hierarchical world view or with a contemporary world view?

Sacramental Celebration: Shaped by Experience in Today's World?

Sacramental celebration can, in principle, be shaped by contemporary events. Any view which holds that liturgy *does* remain unaffected by contemporary events has not taken the history of sacramental life seriously. History indicates that any view which maintains that liturgy *could* remain unaffected by contemporary events is naive. In our own day the church is part of a humanity which lives in a time of such disintegration and destruction that we question whether there is any hope with which to face the future. The disorientation and hopelessness of our own age is nowhere more apparent than in the two holocausts of the twentieth century: the extermination of six million Jews and millions of others at the hands of the Nazis and the threat of nuclear war which would destroy the entire world.[5]

The two holocausts, one fact, the other possibility (or probability), remind us of the powerlessness, meaninglessness, and futurelessness which we often feel but are afraid to face. Each presents a challenge and a call to radical conversion—to a God who is with us in the midst of powerlessness and meaninglessness, and who is already ahead of us, on the other side of the fate that threatens to destroy humanity.

Sacramental celebration is a vital force in the ongoing conversion of the Christian community. But the ongoing conversion of the community does, on the other hand, demand the ongoing conversion of sacramental celebration so that it more adequately addresses the experience of persons.

What would sacramental celebration look like if the twofold holocaust were taken seriously by the Christian community at worship? To introduce prayers of petition that God grant us protection from nuclear war or that we recognize the Jews as forebears of Christian faith hardly tackles the issues of today's world—one shaped by people's experience of the meaninglessness and futurelessness signaled in the twofold holocaust. Instead, for example, more attention might be given to "lamentation" as it is found in the Bible. In homilies Christian hope must be spoken of more soberly: The days when the future of young people looked bright and promising are over. Many young people today even wonder if there will be any future for them, to say nothing of their children's future. Do preachers recognize such problems when they speak of hope and future? For many young people, it is not simply lack of faith which causes them to question the possibility of hope and future. Some have good reason to do so, and they must be addressed in this light.

In the final analysis the hard question—however distasteful to some—is being asked by many: Can those who profess faith in Jesus Christ profess it in face of the twofold holocaust? Whatever the answer, this question must be faced.

The issue of the twofold holocaust is raised as a concrete case that illustrates some of the painful and demanding consequences of taking the connection between sacraments and Christian living seriously. Other issues and questions could be raised to illustrate the point. As a brief example, the words in the Mass: "Take this *all* of you and eat...take this *all* of you and drink." Why are millions dying for want of food and drink? Because the basic necessities of life are withheld from those who need them. *All* do not eat, and *all* do not drink of the fruit of the vine and the work of the human hands.[6] Christian worship and life cannot afford to remain untouched by the events of our age.

The Contemporary Renewal of Sacramental Life and Liturgy

What are the forms of liturgy and Christian life appropriate to our own day? Whatever answer is given, a response which is appropriate for our own age will be influenced by a renewed Christology, ecclesiology, and anthropology.[7] The way we understand Christ, the church, and the human person has changed significantly in the latter part of the twentieth century. In addition to the pastoral and liturgical renewal promoted by Vatican II, there has been a renewal of traditional theology. Theology of the sacraments has not been untouched by this process of revision. Classical sacramental theology, the fruit of a gradual development that began in the Middle Ages, used the Christology, ecclesiology, and anthropology of that time in order to articulate its main insights. The major insights of this traditional, classical approach to the sacraments are not to be disregarded, but a renewed approach to sacramental life and Christian living needs to take seriously contemporary insights regarding Jesus Christ, the church, and the human person which have come to the fore in the life of the church in this century.

The Renewal of Christology

Christology refers to the study and understanding of the meaning and significance of Jesus Christ. Since the council, new insights regarding the meaning and significance of Jesus Christ are due in large measure to biblical research and new methods of interpreting Scripture. Strange though it may seem, one of the great contributions of contemporary Christology is the emphasis placed upon the man Jesus within the Christian mystery. In the not too distant past, preaching, Catholic teaching, and practice gave little attention to the historical person of Jesus of Nazareth. Catholicism prior to the council was in practice focused primarily on God's absolute otherness. One of the great accomplishments of the renewal has been the attention given to the central role of Jesus in Christianity.

A second noteworthy characteristic in many currents of contemporary Christology is the emphasis placed upon the humanity of Jesus. The tradition of the church affirms that Jesus is both truly divine and truly human in one person. Most Christians have little difficulty believing that Jesus is truly divine. The real problem seems to be that many are unable to accept or believe that Jesus is truly human. Contemporary approaches to Christology focus upon the humanity of Jesus as that which reveals the divine. This emphasis is in line with the sacramental vision of reality that is the subject of the present work. First, one looks to the concrete and historical reality. Then one moves from that to what is revealed, disclosed, or signified by means of the concrete and historical reality. In the case at hand, one looks first to Jesus, the man of Nazareth, apparently like any other, and then proceeds, by means of the experience of faith, to uncover what the life, ministry, death and Resurrection of Jesus mean for human beings. It is in this sense that Jesus is spoken of as the basic or primordial sacrament of God by theologian Edward Schillebeeckx in his ground-breaking work in sacramental theology.[8] It is precisely through the humanity of Jesus that his divinity and the mystery of the divine Trinity are revealed.

The recovery of the historical Jesus in Christology requires that

Christian assemblies at worship remember his life and his whole ministry as this is revealed in the Scriptures and in the proclamation of the word. In the sacramental practices of the not-too-distant past, there was a tendency to focus rather narrowly upon the sacrifice of his death in such a way that Jesus' life and ministry were not given due attention. Here the singular importance of the proclamation of the word as a focus in sacramental celebration becomes clear. The understanding of the Eucharist as sacrifice is only properly understood if it is seen within the larger context of the story of Jesus' life and ministry. No single dimension of the Christian mystery—for example, that of sacrifice—can express the fullness of the Lord's presence. No one image, again let us say that of sacrifice, exhausts the depth of his passion. Christian liturgy is bound up with and shaped by word. The proclamation of the word, by which God's presence and action in Jesus Christ are disclosed to the assembly, serves to widen the horizon and to provide a variety of other references to the life and ministry of Jesus. Within this much broader picture his sacrifice may be more properly understood. Hence, in contemporary sacramental celebration, no one image or dimension of the Christian mystery exhausts the full meaning of, or takes priority over, the life and ministry of Jesus which is proclaimed in word and remembered in the breaking of the bread and the sharing of the cup.

The Renewal of Ecclesiology

Ecclesiology refers to the study and understanding of the church. In this area, there have been some monumental shifts in understanding due, in large part, to some of the statements about the nature and mission of the church which emerged as a result of Vatican II. As some of these statements have been developed by contemporary approaches to ecclesiology, the church is less and less understood as primarily hierarchical in nature. In line with Vatican II's vision of the church as the People of God, this view of church stresses its participatory, communal, and collegial nature. A renewed ecclesiology does not speak of the church as the perfect society on earth. Rather, the church is understood as a pilgrim people whose mission is to witness to the coming of God's reign and to its values: justice, mercy, unity, truth, reconciliation, and compassion, among others. From this perspective, the church is herald and servant of the reign of God.

A second important characteristic of contemporary currents in ecclesiology makes the clear distinction between church and God's reign. From this it follows that one may not remain uncritical toward, or assign absolute value to, the ways and means by which the church strives to bring about the reign of God. That is to say, it is the reign or kingdom of God which is of absolute value, not the church. The role of the church is to assist the coming of the reign, or God's intention in the world. The church is not the reign of God. Further, the church itself is not the ultimate judge, but is itself under the judgment of the Lordship of Christ. The church is a sign or sacrament of the reign of God. It is a concrete, historical means by which a deeper reality—the reign of God—is revealed or manifest. It is, however, not identical to the reality signified.

A third characteristic of this renewed ecclesiology, related to the second one, is its view of the church as sign or sacrament, that is, in terms of its significance: what the church signifies to its own members and to the broader human community. A renewed ecclesiology focuses less upon the church as the custodian of power, truth, and holiness, and, more upon the church as the means by which God gives concrete form to divine action on behalf of the whole human race. From this perspective the church is that part of the human race which, in the name of all humanity, responds to God's invitation to the fullness of life.

A result of this renewed view of the church is the recognition of the importance of all the baptized and of their contribution and responsibility for the life and mission of the church. It also demands that the baptized recognize their ministry to one another in such a church.

The Renewal of Christian Anthropology

Anthropology refers to the study of human being. The Christian anthropology which has emerged from the renewal sanctioned by the Second Vatican Council is the fruit of developments in biblical research and advanced methods of scriptural interpretation, as well as philosophical currents such as existentialism, phenomenology, and various studies in human intentionality. This renewed anthropology may be sketched in four points.

First, the human being is understood to be created in the image of God. She or he is a historical, concrete reflection of the divine, a sacrament of the life of God. This is a positive view of the human person, especially when seen in light of some of the negative views of the human person sometimes expressed in the church's sacramental practice prior to Vatican II. To develop and grow into the fullness of God's image, the human being must develop proper relations with God, the world, and other human beings. This positive Christian anthropology has important consequences in the sacramental life of the church: it enables us to see the sacraments as establishing and strengthening human beings in their relationship to God, world, and others, rather than as giving grace to repair a human nature which is considered essentially depraved. This more positive view is in line with the traditional Catholic emphasis on the sanctifying, as well as healing, power of sacraments.

Second, the human person is a historical being. With a focus upon the natural and supernatural, and a very clear difference between the two, much of the world view of the Middle Ages was colored by an understanding of human nature as static and unchanging. Human nature was a "given."

The Jewish setting within which Christianity emerged was very different from this, however. Well before the time of Jesus, the people of Israel placed great emphasis on the historical dimension of the human person. A renewed Christian anthropology has recovered the singular importance of the historical. The human being is part of a history, and history is made up of relations with others in the human community. We do not exist in isolation. Our fulfillment as human beings and as Christians is never a given, never something fully accomplished. It is always something to be attained through progressive formation and ongoing participation in grace and Spirit, which come through community with others sharing a particular historical period. And history changes persons and communities.

Third, a renewed Christian anthropology views the human being as a dynamic reality. From this perspective, the person is a participant in an ongoing process of growth and change. Precisely as God's image, we are endowed with a source of energy that allows us, to a degree, to shape our lives and the life of the human community. In brief, the human person is created with a dynamism which is of divine origin and which enables the person to become more fully what she or he is, the image of God.

Fourth, a renewed anthropology sees the human person as a unity. Even to this day, many speak of the human person as a being made up of various parts. This is due, in large measure, to a dualist conception of the human person, which is rooted in Greek philosophy and which has had great impact upon Christianity. Human being, it held, consists of two parts: body and soul. In the Middle Ages, Thomas Aquinas (d. 1274) envisioned the human person as a unified being with distinct faculties of intellect, will, and sense. Some of his interpreters and some key figures in the French school of Christian spirituality of the seventeenth century did not manage to keep Aquinas's unified vision to the fore. What resulted has come to be called "faculty psychology." From this perspective the human person is viewed as having not merely distinct, but separate faculties of intellect and will.

In this view, the person thinks with the intellect and chooses through an act of the will. Contemporary views of the human person indicate that it is often not so clear cut. The end result of either the dualist approach or the perspective of faculty psychology is a vision of the human person out of keeping with the biblical tradition, where the human person is not understood as the end product of body and soul or the various faculties. Various biblical images convey an understanding of human being as a dynamic unity. The term *heart*, for example, describes the total unity which the person is. When used in the Bible, *heart* (*leb* and *lebab* in the Hebrew, and *kardia* in the Greek) describes the root or source of diverse personal functions. This early usage expressed the whole, total person: the person was not viewed as someone who thinks with the intellect and chooses with the will. Heart describes the person as a whole, open to attraction by others and by God. Many currents in contemporary Christian anthropology have recovered this sense of the person as a unity.

In all three areas, Christology, ecclesiology, and anthropology, dramatic shifts in understanding have occurred. It is now necessary for us to spell out some of the consequences of these contemporary insights for sacramental life and Christian living.

Consequences of Renewed Christology, Ecclesiology, and Anthropology for Sacramental Celebration

If the insights gained from the renewal of Christology, ecclesiology, and anthropology are taken seriously, then several consequences follow. First, our approach to sacramental life will give more attention to the christological and ecclesiological dimensions of the sacraments. The sacraments are expressions and extensions, as it were, of Christ and the church, or better, Christ in the church. In a former day, the focus in the sacraments was upon the priest. But if our renewed Christology and ecclesiology are given their proper due, we come to see that the sacraments exist to give corporate and meaningful expression to Christ's presence in the church and the church's presence in and to Christ. The sacraments are not individual, isolated things. They are expressions of the saving presence that God is through Christ in the church.

Second, in our approach to sacraments greater attention must be given to the human person and his or her experience. This follows from the renewal of Christian anthropology. Allowance must be made for the variety and plurality of social, cultural, and environmental elements which would naturally suggest a variety of liturgical forms. Liturgical forms, at present, do not reflect adequately actual cultural and social pluralism. Further, much is to be learned from the contributions of various sciences which are making significant gains in understanding the nature and function of symbol, the role of ritual in human life, and the various modes of celebration.

Third, the insights in each of the three areas treated help point out the intrinsic connection among the sacraments, Christ, church, and humanity. There is, as a result of a renewed Christology, ecclesiology, and anthropology, a deeper awareness of the relationship between the ways in which people express their relationship with God through Christ in the church's worship, and their living out of what is believed in their dealings with others in the human community. There is a reciprocal relationship between liturgy and life, sacraments and Christian morality.

Appropriate Sacramental Celebration

A contemporary approach to sacramental life and Christian living, informed by the changes we have considered above, requires great attention to the practical implications of what is believed and expressed in worship. In the Eucharist the Christian community expresses its belief in and commitment to the possibility of communion with God and others. It expresses the intention to work for a world in which justice will reign, and the poor and forgotten will hold first place. In the sacrament of penance the Christian community lives out of a new vision of reality, from the perspective of God's mercy and forgiveness. Through baptism one is invited to live a way of life based on the covenant through membership in God's people and through the power of the Spirit. This entails living according to the Spirit and not according to the flesh (Rom. 8): a spirit of childhood, not of fear. The sacrament of anointing of the sick invites us to live in remembrance of Christ's healing ministry which provides new perspective on suffering and death and which encourages the Christian community to care for the sick and to struggle against illness, suffering, and depersonalization.

If the practical implications of sacramental life, as briefly described above, are to be impressed upon the Christian community, then appropriate sacramental celebration is required, not simply desired. Liturgical celebration must itself give expression to the renewed Christology, ecclesiology, and anthropology which we have treated.

Sacramental celebration appropriate to our age takes seriously the truth that the church is the People of God, sacrament of Christ in the world. Before all else, the church is the community of the baptized. Whatever is said of ministry in the church, ordained or nonordained, must be said in this light. This understanding of the church might be called laical (from the Greek *laos*, "people"). This perspective focuses upon persons in community who are the Body of Christ. The keynotes of this understanding of church are the categories of People of God, communion, prophecy, and service, not hierarchy, power, or authority.

Appropriate celebration of the sacraments today would give a great deal of attention to the formative role of the word. Since the Second Vatican Council, increasing attention has been given to the place of the word in liturgy. In the period just prior to the council, the Scriptures did not have a prominent place in the lives of many Roman Catholics. When used in liturgical settings, the word was often used improperly. In contemporary liturgical practice, the proclamation and the hearing of the word are looked upon as manifestations and disclosures of the presence of God. It is in the Scriptures that the community learns the story of Jesus' life and ministry. Appropriate sacramental practice requires that due attention be given to the word as formative of Christian life. As a result, planning and preparation for proclamation, hearing, and preaching must be kept to the fore as singularly important values. In the hearing and proclamation of the word, the community receives and expresses its identity as the Body of Christ, as it does in the breaking of the bread and sharing of the cup, or in the anointing with oil or chrism.

It should be clear from what has been suggested above that the primary symbol in any sacramental celebration is the gathered assembly. The singularly important role of the assembly is described in detail in the *Constitution on the Sacred Liturgy* of the Second Vatican Council (nos. 7, 11, 14, 27).

To take but one example, music should be selected with the assembly in mind. It is to be chosen on the basis of its ability to lift the assembly's mind and heart to God, not simply because it sounds nice or is easily sung. In practice music is sometimes selected because "everyone knows this one," thus requiring little by way of preparation or planning. Music which sounds good may or may not invite the community to participation. Here one must raise the question: Is liturgical music an act of ministry, or service, which invites the prayer and worship of a community, or is it simply a good performance for the pleasure of the congregation? Environment calls the assembly to worship. Music creates environment.

In these days since Vatican II, there has been a tendency to confuse good sacramental celebration with good liturgical music. But good liturgical music is not the same as good sacramental celebration. Strange as it may seem, liturgy requires far more planning, preparation, and know-how by all involved than does first-rate liturgical music. Ordained or nonordained, all liturgical ministry is done from *within* the assembly and *for* the assembly. This means that priests and other liturgical ministers must consider themselves, first of all, as baptized Christians, part of the community that God calls.

From this it follows that the ministry of the presbyter (priest) in presiding at liturgy is a ministry *to* the assembly. Likewise, all other ministries. It is on this base, an apostolic (which implies being sent *to*) and sacramental base, that the sacrament of holy orders rests. Even if one would insist on an essential difference between the priesthood of the ordained and the priesthood of all the baptized, the point remains that the task of all who serve as ministers in the church's liturgy is to serve or minister *to* the assembly.

This kind of thinking demands a breadth of liturgical ministries. It means that there must be a change of mind regarding the role of the assembly. Without this there is no true sacramental celebration and no effective communication of the practical implications of the sacraments for daily Christian living, only those who say Mass and those who attend Mass. Everything, even preaching, has to be affected by this change of mind.

If the primary focus in sacramental celebration is the assembly, then several consequences follow. First, the more people involved in a liturgical service, the more important the coordination of the various ministries. This is the role or job of the presider, or priest. Second, liturgical ministry demands adequate preparation. Third, to preside at liturgy means to have a comprehensive understanding of what is taking place. This cannot be done without touching bases with all the liturgical ministries involved. This is best done by entering into the liturgical planning process.

If it is true, as has been suggested in this chapter, that the sacraments themselves express a Christian view of human life and of the world, and if this is to be communicated to those who celebrate the sacraments, then allowance must be made for a variety of liturgical forms which better enable the Christian community to express and receive its identity as the Body of Christ in today's world.

Notes

1. *Dogmatic Constitution on the Church*, chap. 5, in *The Documents of Vatican II*, ed. Walter M. Abbott (New York: America Press, 1966). All references to the documents of Vatican II are based upon this edition. Hereafter, references to the documents, as well as to Sacred Scripture, will be included in the text. All scriptural references are from *The Jerusalem Bible*.

2. The significance of the notion developed in the council's *Dogmatic Constitution on the Church*, chap. 2, is ably explored by Sandra M. Schneiders, "Evangelical Equality," *Spirituality Today* 38, no. 4 (Winter 1986): 293–302.

3. For an excellent analysis of the way in which the period of Christian origins is sometimes imagined as a "golden age," see Robert L. Wilken, *The Myth of Christian Beginnings* (Garden City, NY: Doubleday, 1971), p. 18ff.

4. The term *reign of God* is preferable to *kingdom of God* for several reasons. Among these, the term *reign* better expresses the active nature of God's intention coming to be in the world. The term *kingdom* often carries the connotation of place and space, as if God's kingdom were a sort of cosmic playground or glorified geographical location.

5. This theme has been treated at length in Michael Downey, "Worship Between the Holocausts," *Theology Today* 43, no. 1, (April 1986): 75–87. The issue is also treated in John Pawlikowski, "Worship after the Holocaust: An Ethician's Reflections," *Worship* 58, no. 4 (July 1984): 315–29.

6. For a fuller treatment of this point, see Monika Hellwig, *The Eucharist and the Hunger of the World* (New York: Paulist Press, 1976).

7. On this point, I am indebted to the insights of Raymond Vaillancourt, *Toward a Renewal of Sacramental Theology* (Collegeville, MN: Liturgical Press, 1979).

8. Edward Schillebeeckx, *Christ the Sacrament of the Encounter with God* (New York: Sheed & Ward, 1963).

2

Sign, Symbol, Sacrament, and Sacramentality

Chapter 1 charted our course; chapter 2 begins our exploration into the very "stuff" of the sacraments. Our aim is not simply to understand the seven sacraments of Roman Catholicism, but the broader notion of sacramentality itself. Ultimately the Christian is called upon to look at all created realities, gestures, actions, and words as expressions of God's life and presence, at least potentially. To do so is not to see the seven sacraments as dispensable or less important. It is rather to see in the seven sacraments a particular or unique manifestation of God's life and presence—a presence loose in the world and in all of human life. In short, we are speaking of a world shot through with God's presence and gifts.

Some Helpful Terms

To begin, it may be helpful to define a few terms which are used frequently in these pages: rite, ritual, worship, liturgy, and grace.

Rite and Ritual

Rite and ritual are closely related. They refer to a prescribed, approved, and accepted form of words, gestures, and activities which regulate or facilitate a ceremony.

Often these terms are thought to describe only religious ceremonies or services, but if we look more closely we see that rituals are part of the many facets of our lives. Recall the above definition and consider that most families in the United States conduct themselves in quite similar fashion on Thanksgiving, even though there is no uniform ritual for its observation. Remembering and thanking form the whole purpose of Thanksgiving Day. In most homes the ritual consists of gathering people together, eating certain kinds of foods—the almost sacrosanct turkey—recalling stories of former Thanksgivings or stories of the year gone by, and being thankful. Households which do not usually say grace or blessing before meals often do stumble through a sincere prayer of blessing before the Thanksgiving meal. All of these are ingredients of the Thanksgiving ritual, to which are added elements peculiar to each household or family.

Other examples of ritual include birthday celebrations and weddings. In some homes the ritual of birthday celebration includes the honoree's selection of his or her favorite cake, baked specially for the occasion. Aside from the ceremony of marriage itself, wedding celebrations include the toast by the best man, throwing and catching the bride's bouquet, and the couple's first dance to their favorite song. None of these are actually part of the rite or ritual of marriage, but we are inclined to say that "something's missing" if these elements are absent.

The examples above simply aim to illustrate the many different rituals with which we live and to suggest that sacramental rites or rituals are like these in some ways and serve a similar function. Admittedly they are more formalized, and in a way more important to us, because they are more directly concerned with God's presence in our world, human life, history, and church. But a deep appreciation of sacramental rites and rituals is hard to come by without attention to and appreciation of the rites and rituals which form the fabric of our daily lives.[1]

Worship

In addition to the rituals of daily or ordinary life, there are those which regulate or facilitate a ceremony of worship. Worship may be described as a composite act comprised of words, song, gestures, and activities by means of which a person or group gives praise and thanks to God. In using the term *worship* we are referring to all those formal and informal, written and unwritten, spontaneous and prescribed words and actions by which Christians encounter and are encountered by God in assemblies of the church.[2]

Liturgy

Liturgy is a term closely related to worship. It refers to a rite or body of rites by means of which an assembly conducts its public worship. To speak of liturgy is to speak of communal worship or a communal religious service, which is patterned, predictable, purposeful, and public in nature.[3] When capitalized, the term *Liturgy* usually refers to the rite of the Eucharist. Liturgy is not a passive thing, nor is rite or ritual. Liturgy, rite, and ritual are what they are because they are enacted. A ritual in a book of rites is nothing more than ink on paper, just as the words of the prophets are dead letters when not proclaimed, heard, and acted upon. Letters on paper are God's word spoken through the prophets when they are read, heard, proclaimed, and lived. In the same way, liturgy, ritual, or rite can only be properly understood in an active sense.

Grace

Another term which is closely linked to an understanding of sacraments and liturgy is *grace*. For many, grace is understood primarily as a quantitative reality. We get it if we go to church on Sunday, we lose it if we don't. Properly understood, grace is primarily God's own life communicated to human beings. It also refers to God's gift of self. From this perspective we can say that sacraments are not so much a transfer of grace as unique and particular expressions of God's gift of self and our active, communal response to it in Jesus Christ.

A Description of Symbol

In describing sign, symbol, sacrament, and sacramentality we come to a crucial point in our investigation. When we speak of symbol and its relation to sacrament, we often rely on a rather naive understanding of both symbol and sign. Some contemporary approaches, which are based rather exclusively upon an understanding of the root of the word *symbol* (Greek: *sym-ballein*, "to throw together") and a traditional understanding of a sign as something which points to a deeper reality than itself, do not tackle the problem. Both sign and symbol, and their relation to one another, are far more complex than simple definitions might suggest.

David Power offers a thorough analysis of the nature and function of symbol and relates this to an understanding of Christian liturgy.[4] Based on studies of symbol in the fields of theology, philosophy, anthropology, sociology, and various other disciplines, and influenced by the insights of Antoine Vergote, Power understands symbols as concrete signs, gestures, or actions which

> belong within a given cultural context, bear of repetition without being rigid stereotypes, meet affective needs of meaning and belonging, express group identity, even though some are more immediately related to the group and others to the individual, and

are subject to the changes that come with the evolution of time, moving perspectives and changing values.[5]

With this understanding in mind, we could speak of Christian symbols, whether it be breaking bread and sharing the cup, pouring or immersing in water, lighting and carrying candles, as concrete signs, gestures, and actions which express the meaning and truth of the Christian community as the Body of Christ, and through which the community receives its identity as the Body of Christ.

Sacraments Are Symbols?

To many Catholics the terms *sacrament* and *symbol* seem contradictory. According to a traditional definition, a sacrament is an outward *sign* instituted by Christ to give grace. Not too long ago, Catholic grade schoolers were instructed that we (Catholics) believe that the Eucharist is real, while they (Protestants) say its *only* a symbol. The difficulty with this view is twofold. First, it grossly oversimplifies whatever differences there may be between Roman Catholic and Protestant approaches to the Eucharist. Second, it is based upon an incorrect understanding of both sign and symbol.

Sign and Symbol: Similarities and Differences

Often when we use the word *sign* we mean something that refers to a reality beyond itself. A stop sign means or refers to something beyond itself: motionlessness. This can be said of concrete things, actions, gestures, and even words. All may refer to something beyond themselves. If this is what one understands sign to mean then symbols fall into the category of sign. In a more particular sense, however, symbol and sign have come to be distinguished from one another. The difference between them is that while signs have to do with the world as *manageable and functional*, symbols have to do with the world as *meaningful and valuable*. Aidan Kavanagh has written about this difference:

> Symbols, being roomy, allow many different people to put them on, so to speak, in different ways. Signs do not. Signs are unambiguous because they exist to give precise information. Symbols coax one into a swamp of meaning and require one to frolic in it. Symbol is rarely found among the inactive, the obtuse, the confused, or the dull. Signs are to symbols what infancy is to adulthood, what stem is to flower, and the flowering of maturity takes time.[6]

Sign or Symbol? Determined by Context

The difference between sign and symbol is not always so sharp. The meaning of any word, thing, or action is determined in large part by the situation or context in which the word is said, the thing is used, or the action done. For our purposes, there are basically three contexts within which the meaning and significance of words, things, and actions are shaped.[7]

First, in the world of common sense, ordinary, day-in, day-out affairs, words, things, and actions should have direct and straightforward meanings. Ambiguity and multiplicity of meanings are to be avoided as far as possible. Stop signs mean don't go—nothing more, nothing less, nothing else. A vacancy sign which is lit up, or a sign which says that the apartment is for rent means precisely that. Inquiring persons are disappointed, indeed they feel deceived, to learn that in fact the apartment will be for rent only later in the month, or that the occupant of the "vacant" room is not quite ready to leave.

Second, in the world of science, what is said and done may be more theoretical and abstract, but meanings are nonetheless clear and precise. Multiplicity of meanings is undesirable. H_2O is the designation for water and no other composition. $A+B=C$ or $3+5=8$ offer little room for interpretation.

Third, in the context of the symbolic, or poetic, however, many possible meanings are communicated through concrete signs, gestures, or actions. A kiss, a handshake, an invitation to dinner can mean many things. For example, college and university commencement exercises serve to remind graduating students and their families and friends of the past four years spent at such and such an illustrious institution. Commencement exercises are also aimed at cultivating in everyone present a feeling of loyalty and ongoing commitment to the school. They are also designed to let the students know that, yes, in fact college days are now over, and the future awaits them. The ceremony serves an obvious function, that is, the awarding of degrees so that the graduates can assume their appropriate roles as qualified participants in their chosen fields. But the whole situation or context is symbolic.

Again, it is situation or context which shapes the significance of concrete signs, gestures, and actions. Giving a piece of paper can mean very little. But when this action is done within the context of commencement exercises, with all its pomp and ceremony, it bears great meaning and significance.

The same can be said for words. Their meaning is shaped by the context in which they are used. The word *needle* may refer to that metallic instrument with which clothes are sewn and mended, *or* something being done which irritates another ("Stop needling me!"). Or it may have still another meaning if, for example, the spiritual attitude of the Christian is described by using the term in the gospel passage: "It is harder for the rich one to enter the reign of God than for a camel to pass through the eye of a needle."

Briefly then, it may be helpful to state at this point that the concrete signs, gestures, actions, and words which form the heart of the sacramental life of the church are symbolic realities. The third context, as described above, is where sacraments and liturgy belong. They have to do with meaning and value. Sacraments are not mere signs, whose purpose is to relay precise information.

Sacraments are Symbols

This difference between sign and symbol is not always as plain as one might be led to think, but it is helpful to keep the distinction in mind. Signs have to do with the useful or functional, symbols have to do with the meaningful and valuable. From this perspective, rather than being *less real* than signs, symbols are *more real*, if you will, than simple signs. Beyond the world of functional signs there lies the far more complex reality of symbol: a concrete object, action, gesture, or word, the purpose of which is to bring about interpersonal communion and communication. In a Christian context, the symbolic realities of liturgy and sacrament are intended to bring about communion and communication among persons and between them and the personal God who is disclosed or revealed in Jesus Christ.

Many may still be inclined to resist speaking of sacraments as symbols and rely upon the former definition of sacrament as an outward *sign* instituted by Christ to give grace. The definition is helpful, indeed, and in fact not in conflict with what has been said of the symbolic nature of sacrament and liturgy. As we have seen above, a symbol lies within the general category of sign and is not opposed to or in a completely separate category from sign. But when considered specifically, symbol is a much richer and more complex reality than sign.

Given a proper understanding of symbol, then, sacraments may be described as symbols of God's presence in world, life, history, and church. The question of the similarities and differences between sacraments and other symbols will be taken up later in this chapter.

Two Characteristics of Symbol

A symbol is a rich and complex reality. Of the many character-istics of symbol, two are treated here. An understanding of these characteristics makes possible a fuller appreciation of the sacraments as symbolic in nature.

Symbol's Many Meanings

Symbols are used in contexts where what is aimed at is the communication of a multiplicity of meanings. Yet more often than not people try to tie down the meaning and significance of a symbol to just one meaning. This is particularly true of the symbolic realities called sacraments. Liturgy and sacraments suffer when people try to restrict their meaning to a uniform, preconceived understanding.

In the ritual of baptism we must recognize what is meant by the word *water* and by the reality of water itself. At one level, the meaning of water is clear and direct. Water is an element not to be confused with tortilla chips or a bacon, lettuce, and tomato sandwich. It quenches thirst, cleanses, and refreshes. But the significance of water in the ritual of baptism has everything to do with the ways in which water communicates a network of various and related mean-ings. It is properly understood when considered in light of the water which was divided from the dry land in the creation story, and the water which flooded all creation except Noah, his wife, and all those on board. There is the water of the divided Red Sea, and the water gushing from the staff-stricken rock. In the New Testament there is the water of Jordan and that of the wedding feast at Cana. There is the water requested of Jesus by the Samaritan woman so that she might drink it. There is the living water which Jesus provided, and there is the cup of water to be given to the thirsty in his name. A number of these meanings are in fact mentioned in the blessing of the baptismal waters.

But, if the waters of baptism are seen, as they often are, only as a means of cleansing from original sin, then the multiple possibilities of meaning are lost. There is a kind of "selective forgetting" of the many meanings of the baptismal ritual in favor of one, and often only one, meaning. Such a tendency does not do justice to the richness of the nature of baptism. This is not to suggest that the notions of stain, blemish, and the inheritance of sin are unimportant, but that when proper attention is given to the other meanings associated with water, the full meaning of baptism is better communicated. Taken all together they invite the Christian community to see in the ritual of baptism a glimpse of the truth of the reality of coming into a world deeply affected by human sinfulness and of the absolute necessity of God's gracious forgiveness.

In the practice of baptism, a sprinkle of water will do, if the primary concern is one of cleansing from sin, which is understood as some sort of invisible blemish on the unseen soul. This concern reflects a type of understanding in which there is a deep separation between the real and the symbolic. What is *really real*, according to this perspective, is the invisible stain on the soul. The stain is understood to be effectively removed through the priestly powers of one whose own soul is understood to have gone through another sort of invisible change at ordination. From this view, attention is drawn to the symbol of water only in reference to how the water veils or hides the deeper, more mysterious cleaning of the blemished soul. The use of water, in this view, seems almost unnecessary. But this is a very different attitude from the sacramental vision which accepts the symbol itself as that which communicates or discloses the divine presence. The many layers of meaning collapse into one, symbolic sensitivity is denied, and in the end, the liturgy and sacraments demeaned, when water is sprinkled sparingly in baptism and not lavishly poured or set in a pool for immersing the infant or adult. Further, in liturgical practice in general, the same problems occur when the fullness and richness of the symbolic nature of sacramental celebration is forsaken in the name of practical pastoral consider-ations, for example, withholding the eucharistic cup because there are too many people, or because some are unjustifiably concerned about the communication of viruses or disease through sharing the cup.

If there are "too many people," the practical solution is to call upon more people to minister more cups of consecrated wine. Common sense suggests that the cup of consecrated wine should not be withheld from an assembly which has just previously heard the words, "Take this *all* of you and drink," spoken over the cup.

Too often in sacramental practice, we do not allow the symbols to "speak" for themselves. We have a tendency to tell them what they can mean. This is to say, they become manipulated. We go to church with minds made up about how God can speak to us, or what God can give us. Further, we have decided what cannot or should not be said or done. It would be helpful in sacramental practice to say what is meant, and mean what is said. Again, to cite the example of the cup of wine—should anyone say, "Take this *all* of you and drink from it," if all do not have the opportunity to drink? If, like the cup, this bread is given "for you and for all," then all should eat of the one loaf of bread. Liturgy breaks down when the bread which is spoken of as given for all is not eaten by anyone but the priest, and everyone else in the assembly is served from consecrated bread kept in the tabernacle.

In the end, the challenge is to permit the symbols to stand forth in all their richness and fullness, attending to the many meanings disclosed or communicated in and through them. More importantly, the Christian community needs to hear less about sacraments veiling or hiding God's presence—God, it is insisted, is *really* present, all appearances to the contrary. We need to grow in confidence and unabashed conviction that we can look to the symbols themselves for a revelation of God's presence in as simple a gesture as anointing with healing oil, or in the blessing and sharing of such simple and basic elements as food and drink.[8]

Symbol and Symbolized: Respecting the Difference

In the symbolic context, concrete signs, gestures, actions, and words help bring about communication and communion among persons. Interpersonal communion and communication depend upon the symbolic, and in fact are symbolic by nature.

By virtue of the nature and function of symbol, there are limitations on the communication and communion which the symbol brings about. A reality which is communicated in symbol is given in a form distinct from the reality itself. The very purpose of symbol is to allow realities *not* present in their own mode or form to be made present. For example, a man's love for a woman is expressed in the form of the giving of a rose. There is a difference between the reality symbolized (love) and the symbol (giving a rose) which communicates or manifests it. Although the existence of his love is distinct from the symbol, without the symbol the reality of love may lie dormant or become a mere abstraction. Presence in and through symbol is mediated presence: love is mediated through the symbol of giving a rose. Mediated presence is not any less real, but there is a difference, a distinction, between the reality symbolized and the symbol itself. The two are not identical, and the reality symbolized can never be fully expressed in any one symbol.

To receive and express meaning and truth in and through symbol, and to allow the symbolic to reveal and effect communication and communion, one must recognize this difference and embrace what is not given in and through symbol, as well as what is. To cite our example again, if the woman is to appreciate and receive the gift of the man's love symbolized in the rose, she must recognize that his love is much more than a rose, even though she receives his love, in this example, precisely through the giving of the rose.

A consideration of what is involved in human work and in sexuality may help to clarify what is at issue here. Through work a person finds and expresses self-knowledge and identity.[9] Self-knowledge is not gained primarily through introspection and reflection upon the self alone, but rather by the creative expression of the self by means of constructive actions, language, and the imagination. The artist Basil Hallward in Oscar Wilde's *The Picture of Dorian Gray* may serve as an example. Basil's work was a fine and accurate portrayal of the youthful and handsome Dorian. But Basil himself realizes that the work of his brush is far more a projection and expression of himself than anything else. The influence, energy, and force unleashed in Basil's work are seen in the effect which Basil's work, the portrait of Dorian Gray, has upon the life of its subject, Dorian, and all those touched by him.

Vital as work may be to the process of self-knowledge and self-identity, the human person lives an illusion if one's self is confused with one's work. Though one is constantly expressing self and learning of oneself through work, the person is never identical with the work. There is a difference between who one is and what one does.

When considering human sexuality it is also important to keep this type of distinction in mind. Through sexual intimacy the human person gives of self and receives of another. In such communion between persons self-knowledge and self-identity develop. Persons become who they are through self-expression in the many forms which sexual intimacy may take. That is to say that there are many degrees and types of sexual self-expression, not all of which involve genital expression. The acceptance of one's sexuality, and the expression of oneself through it, are necessary and unavoidable steps in the process of self-knowledge and personal identity. But illusion creeps in again when one's self is equated with one's sexuality. The person's deepest self is always distinct from, and indeed more than, the sexual expression of that self. Persons identified primarily in terms of sexual orientation, masses of persons consumed by anxiety about sexual performance, and the seemingly unbridled quest for sexual experimentation—all give evidence of the tendency to confuse the distinction between the person and his or her sexuality, and the inability or unwillingness to recognize the nonidentity between the two.

In both work and sexuality, one's self is both received and given.

That is to say, one expresses the self, and simultaneously receives knowledge and identity—who one is—precisely through such self-giving. It is common enough to speak of giving oneself in both. But even in the most intimate act of sexual union, something of the self, the deepest part of the self, is unavailable to the other. In communion and communication between persons, even of the most intimate sort, there is a degree of absence in the very expression of presence. Real exchange, communication, and communion among persons cannot be achieved unless there is a recognition that the totality of the other person is not exhausted in self-expression through sexuality or work.

The nonidentity of symbol and symbolized is basic to sacrament and liturgy. No symbol of God's presence can be understood as expressing, communicating, or giving the total reality of God or the fullness of the divine presence. Each symbol of the holy finds its place alongside others in a whole network or schema of sacred symbols and images. One symbol cannot do justice to the reality of Jesus' presence and the memory of his passion, death and Resurrection. The symbols of the Lord's presence in sacramental action, for example, breaking bread and sharing cup, are inextricably linked to those of the divine presence in the assembly or community. What is more, the symbols of Jesus' presence find their place together with the symbols which communicate the presence of the Spirit. Finally, the sacramental actions themselves are only properly understood in relation to narrative and doxology, which are the vocal prayers, or words through which God's action in history is recalled, God's presence is invoked in the present, and by which God is thanked and praised.

The whole network of symbols consists of a multiplicity of forms which are intended to communicate the various modes of God's presence. Even when taken as a whole, the totality of symbols of the holy are quite incapable of communicating the fullness of the reality of God's being in the world, and humanity's being in God. Any religious group must recognize that its own claims to truth and to life's ultimate meaning are partial and necessarily limited. The same must be said of the group's symbol system. The Christian community celebrates faith in Christ and the Spirit through a whole network of symbols; at the same time Christians must remain aware that there is a difference between the symbols of God's presence in world, human life, history, and church, and the fullness of that divine presence. Celebration of faith in Christ and Spirit through word and sacrament must stir up in us a deeper longing and a profound respect for what is not fully given, communicated, or disclosed in word and sacrament, as well as a deep appreciation for what is.

Some Practical Problems

These two characteristics of the symbolic, the multiplicity of meaning communicated in symbol and the difference between symbol and symbolized, pose serious difficulties for a good number of Roman Catholics. In the first case, many would insist that the Eucharist, for example, is the Body and Blood of Christ. For them that is what it means. Nothing less, nothing more, nothing else. Eucharist means one thing, not many. Hence faithful churchgoers present themselves for worship week after week with minds made up beforehand about what the eucharistic celebration is and means. As it were, they have decided what God can and cannot give and be in the eucharistic celebration. Attention to the multiplicity of meaning communicated in and through symbol requires that persons and communities look to the symbols as rich and complex realities which disclose God's presence in new, surprising, and manifold ways. Here, the role of imagination is central, but well beyond the limits of our present investigation.[10]

The nonidentity of symbol and symbolized is more perplexing still for many Roman Catholics. Many are of the mind that in the Eucharist the bread is Jesus and Jesus is the bread. This is affirmed by many, and supported by a very naive reading of church teaching, especially the doctrine of transubstantiation. To recall our earlier example, to suggest that the bread is Jesus and Jesus is the bread is like saying that giving a rose is my love and my love is giving a rose: it does not recognize that the presence of Jesus is given in a form other than himself, just as love is expressed or communicated in a form other than itself.

Transubstantiation, as affirmed by Thomas Aquinas and other theologians, is an attempt to explain the real presence of Christ in the Eucharist. Transubstantiation, properly understood, does not affirm a physical but a sacramental presence of Christ in the Eucharist: a type of presence communicated symbolically. It is presence that is nonetheless real.

Aquinas's interpreters were not quite as clever as he was, and transubstantiation often came to be interpreted and explained as real, therefore physical, presence. As a result, a good number of persons who have learned something about transubstantiation find themselves rather preoccupied by the question of how Jesus gets *into* the little white piece of bread.

Many view the sacraments, especially the Eucharist, from this rather naive physicalist perspective. I am reminded of a middle-aged student who came to my office a few weeks after enrollment in my course on sacraments. She explained her sense of overwhelming confusion at these notions of multiplicity of meaning and nonidentity between symbol and symbolized. For her, the notion of nonidentity seemed to undermine the whole reality of the sacraments. Upon asking her the meaning of the sacraments, she quickly explained that, when she was a girl she had been taught that the presence of Christ in the Eucharist was real in such a way that if she bit or chewed the consecrated bread, it would bleed in her mouth. Further, she was told that if she believed strongly enough, at the elevation of the consecrated bread she would be able to see the infant Jesus moving around in it.

These may seem gross exaggerations, and some may inquire about their usefulness in a treatment of sacraments. But it is helpful to see the degree to which an understanding of real presence has been misinterpreted and misrepresented, thus explaining to some degree why a proper comprehension of sacramental presence is difficult for some to accept.

Celebrated in and through Christian Symbols: The Presence of the Risen Christ

At the core of these difficulties with the view of sacrament treated here is a misconception about what is being celebrated in the sacramental life of the church. What is claimed to be present in the Christian community, in word and sacrament, is the presence of the risen Christ, not the physical, historical Jesus of Nazareth.

The nature of the Resurrection itself or of the risen Christ is not immediately apparent in the New Testament writings; the nature of the risen body is not clear. The New Testament itself presents a variety of images and stories which describe Jesus' abiding presence with the disciples after his death. The very variety of images and stories itself illustrates that the nature of the risen Christ is unable to be captured in any one description. Taken all together they suggest only that Jesus has been taken up into a radically new dimension of existence, yet he remains present to his disciples. It is a presence at once too difficult to describe precisely, yet too deeply experienced to be denied. But it is clear from a thorough reading of the New Testament that what is being communicated in the images and stories of the risen Christ is not simply the continuation of his physical, material body beyond death.

Resurrection is not the resuscitation of a corpse. It is a radical transformation and entry into a new level of being beyond the limits of space and time. The same faith which affirms that Jesus has been lifted up, glorified, exalted, raised to a new and radically different mode of existence at God's right hand, affirms that he is with us, present to us, until the end of time. It is this presence of the risen Christ alive in the church through the power of the Spirit which is celebrated in word and sacrament in the Eucharist and in the whole sacramental life of the church.

Sacraments and Other Symbols: Similarities and Differences

What, if any, is the difference between the sacraments and other symbols? A frequent response to this question is: "The sacraments were instituted by Christ to give grace. That's the primary difference!" But to suggest that the institution of the seven sacraments by Jesus is the basis for their difference from all other symbols is not very helpful.

That Jesus instituted the sacraments is not disputed. The question is *how* they were instituted. To institute means to begin, to initiate, or to establish. As research in the fields of biblical studies and liturgical studies comes up with new and fresh insights, it becomes increasingly clear that Jesus did not lay out a blueprint for the development of the sevenfold sacramental system of Roman Catholicism. Jesus did not give specific instructions for the establishment of this or that sacrament. Nor do we know exactly what he intended by what is said in certain passages of the New Testament which have often been cited as proof-texts for the institution of this or that sacrament.

Rather than trying to guarantee that the sacraments were instituted by Christ in a very narrow sense, we need to view the question of institution in light of the whole life, death and Resurrection of Jesus. The sacramental life of the church finds its origin in the entire mystery of Jesus Christ. The issue of the institution of the sacrament of anointing then becomes a question of looking at the whole healing ministry of Jesus and its continuation in the life of the church, rather than trying to support the claim that Jesus intended to begin, or institute, the sacrament of anointing by appealing to this or that New Testament passage. It is increasingly difficult to support the position that the sacrament of Christian marriage was instituted by Jesus at the wedding feast of Cana, since, until the eleventh century, Christian marriage was not viewed as a separate sacrament alongside six others, and there was no clearly defined Christian wedding ritual. It is now more commonly recognized that Jesus' view of the proper relationship between man and woman, and consequently his view of marriage, is more readily discerned by looking at the way Jesus treated women and related to them, rather than by a narrow focus on some doubtful incident of institution—like Cana. This latter type of approach is precisely what has been discredited by contemporary biblical and liturgical studies.

Our purpose is to develop a vision of sacraments which views sacraments within the wider horizon of sacramentality. All created realities, gestures, actions, and words, from this perspective, may be expressions of God's life and presence. Such a broadening of horizon requires that when considering the question of institution, the focus is upon the entire life, ministry, passion, death and Resurrection of Jesus, not just upon this or that particular moment or event in his life.

Similarities

A wedding ring or, better, the exchange and wearing of wedding rings are highly symbolic activities. They symbolize the love and fidelity of a man and a woman for and to one another until death. But neither the wedding rings nor their exchange contain or fully embody the love and fidelity of the couple. The ring is simply a concrete object. Used in a symbolic setting or context (the marriage ceremony), this band of gold does not itself contain or fully embody love and fidelity. Yet when worn by a husband or wife, a wedding ring causes each spouse to remember the other whose love and fidelity are communicated by the wearing of the ring; their mutual promise and offer of self are perceived as present realities. As a result, one does not hear reference to a wedding ring as *just* a symbol or *only* a symbol. If one uses *only* and *just* as modifiers for the noun *symbol*, then one has not understood the nature and function of symbol as we have been describing it.

The seven sacraments of the Roman Catholic tradition do not differ from the example above, inasmuch as they too are symbolic realities. They are concrete, material things, actions, gestures accompanied by words which are used in a symbolic context. Their purpose is to bring about interpersonal communion and communication. Sacraments do not exist in a completely separate category, a wholly other orbit, as it were, from the other rich symbols with which we live and which touch our lives at a very deep level. Sacraments are only properly appreciated when they are seen as a part of the larger human story.

Differences

Though inseparable from the other rich symbols with which we live, the sacraments are distinct and different from other symbols. Again, they do not differ inasmuch as they are symbols. But they do differ in that sacraments are *symbols of God's presence in world, life, history, and church* (chaps. 4 through 7 below).

Briefly, how are the seven sacraments different from other symbols? In the reality they symbolize, not in their being symbols. Breaking bread symbolizes that we, though many, are one Body in Christ. University commencement exercises do not symbolize or communicate this mystery. The pouring of the waters of baptism and the sealing of the Spirit with chrism symbolize our incorporation into the Body of Christ by grace, and our enlightenment or illumination to do the truth in love freely by the empowerment of the Holy Spirit. A birthday celebration means or signifies something else. A birthday party and the Eucharist—each has its own ritual. Indeed each is a celebration, with accepted and approved ways of doing things. Each is a form of thanksgiving. Yet no one would claim that a birthday celebration is a sacrament of the church.

A Principle of Sacramentality

From what has been said above, one might be inclined to ask whether the seven sacraments of Roman Catholicism are the only symbols of God's presence in world, life, history, and church. Drawing upon the insight of Edward Schillebeeckx, we can see that sacrament is a much broader reality than we might have once thought.[11] Based on his work in sacramental theology we can articulate what may be referred to as a principle of sacramentality, that is, a guiding conviction which shapes all thought and understanding of the reality of sacrament. Such a principle can help clarify why and how a magnificent sunset or sexual intimacy may be called sacramental, while at the same time maintaining the distinct and unique place of the sevenfold sacramental system for the Catholic Christian community.

A principle of sacramentality may be articulated as follows: whenever or wherever a supernatural or invisible reality is realized (made real) historically (in time and space) through action, gesture, word, or material object, that is sacrament. Sacrament is the point of connection between the invisible and the visible, the intangible and the tangible. In sacrament we discern that for which we long in and through that which is given. It is the point of encounter with God and human persons in community. By means of sacrament, we are touched and aroused in our desire to be near the One who is always before us, ahead of us, inviting us into the promised future, precisely through words, gestures, actions, and material things, but who cannot be bound by or contained within them.

Levels of Sacramentality

We may identify three distinct levels of sacramentality.

Jesus, Sacrament of God

For Schillebeeckx, Christ's humanity is the primordial sacrament. God, who is invisible and intangible, always ahead of and before us, has become visible and tangible, near us in Jesus. God's speech, God's Word which is wisdom, has become flesh in the person of Jesus of Nazareth, who is proclaimed Lord. This concrete, historical person is for Christian faith *the* symbol of God's presence in world, life, history, and the community of faith. Jesus Christ is understood as the first and most basic sacrament; through his humanity the Christian community encounters the divine.

Church, Sacrament of Christ

A second level of sacramentality is that of the church, the community of faith and discipleship, brought about by the risen Christ. The cross and Resurrection of Jesus together disclose to some measure the mystery of the radical transformation of his existence into a way of being which transcends, breaks beyond, the limits of time and space. Jesus of Nazareth is no longer physically present. Yet faith affirms that he is at once at God's right hand, glorified, and he is present among us. It is through the church, the concrete, historical community of faith and discipleship, that Christ is present in and to the world through the Spirit. The church is itself the Body of Christ in space and time ever since the time of the death of Jesus. The church is the continuation and extension of Jesus Christ throughout the centuries. Through the flesh and bones of its members, the invisible, intangible God is made visible, concrete, and comes near. In the humanity of Jesus the divine is revealed. Jesus is God's sacrament; the church is Christ's sacrament, for in the concrete, historical body of the church, Christ is visible.

The Sacraments of the Church

It is on these bases, Christ as primary sacrament and the church as symbol or sacrament of Christ, that the sevenfold sacramental system of Roman Catholicism rests. They are unintelligible otherwise. The sacraments exist, then, at a third degree or level of sacramentality. The first two provide the very possibility of the existence of the seven sacraments. We might envision the sacraments as a continuation of the mystery of the Incarnation by which the invisible and intangible God draws near through Christ *in* the church. The sacrament of anointing, for example, is an extension of the church's care for the sick, and its struggle against illness, suffering, and depersonalization.

But the church's care for the sick is itself a continuation of Christ's healing ministry which helps us to view suffering and death in a new light. Through the ministry of healing entrusted to the church, the full meaning of which is expressed in sacramental anointing, the healing ministry of Jesus continues. He has no hands but ours.

Briefly then, the anointing of the sick (a sacrament of church—level three) is rooted in the care of the sick by the church (sacrament of Christ—level two), which is rooted in the healing ministry of Christ (sacrament of God—level one).

Christian Sacramental Living

What follows from the principle of sacramentality and the various levels of sacramentality is that the notion of sacrament does not apply exclusively to the seven sacraments of Roman Catholicism. Christ is the primordial sacrament of God. The church is the sacrament of Christ's presence in and to the world. In the seven sacraments the presence of the risen Christ in the church is manifest. But this does not exclude the possibility of God's communication and presence in other ways. Indeed, God's grace, God's self-communication, gifts, and presence are loose in the world, and cannot be contained in or confined to the sacramental rites of a religious group. But Roman Catholics have priorities among the great and gracious mysteries of life. This requires that some symbols will be more valued and treasured, more central to the task of being and becoming Christian. It is for this reason that the seven sacraments came to be distinguished from the other symbols with which we live.[12]

The seven sacraments are a continuing manifestation of God's presence in the world, life, history, and the church. They are focal symbols of God's presence, central to the task of being and becoming

Christian. But these actions, gestures, concrete things, and words cannot be viewed as the only sacramental realities in the life of the Catholic Christian. To be Christian, to be baptized into a covenant community which finds its true home at the table of the Lord, is to live sacramentally. Here we can speak of yet a *fourth level of sacramentality*: Christian sacramental living. Christ's presence in the church, manifest in the seven sacraments, is present and active in the lives of each and every one who lives in his Spirit. All life and all human activity have the possibility of disclosing the presence of the God who has come near in Jesus and who abides with us through the Spirit. Our concrete lives, our seemingly insignificant actions, our gestures, and our words are themselves sacramental, or can become so. It is through them that the divine is present in the world and active in history.

Notes

1. For a useful introductory treatment of this relationship, see Tad Guzie, *The Book of Sacramental Basics* (New York: Paulist Press, 1981), chap. 1.

2. William H. Willimon, *The Service of God: Christian Work and Worship* (Nashville: Abingdon Press, 1983), pp. 16–17.

3. Ibid., p. 17.

4. David N. Power, *Unsearchable Riches: The Symbolic Nature of Liturgy* (New York: Pueblo Publishing Co., 1984).

5. Ibid., p. 62.

6. Aidan Kavanagh, *Elements of Rite* (New York: Pueblo Publishing Co., 1982), p. 5.

7. Power, *Unsearchable Riches*, pp. 64–65.

8. Ibid., p. 56.

9. A thorough treatment of this is found in John Paul II's encyclical *Laborem Exercens* (14 September 1981). See Gregory Baum, *The Priority of Labor: A Commentary on Laborem Exercens, Encyclical Letter of Pope John Paul II* (New York: Paulist Press, 1982).

10. For more on the role of imagination in liturgy, see Patrick Collins, *More Than Meets the Eye* (New York: Paulist Press, 1983).

11. Edward Schillebeeckx, *Christ the Sacrament of the Encounter with God* (New York: Sheed & Ward, 1963).

12. Guzie, *The Book of Sacramental Basics*, p. 51.

3

Historical Overview of the Sacramental Life of the Church

The aim of the historical survey of this chapter is to throw light upon our present efforts to understand the sacraments and to see the connection between sacramental celebration and Christian living, from their roots in history.

Attention will be given to seven focal points: the origins of Christian sacramentality within Judaism; the New Testament period; the patristic period; the Middle Ages; the Reformation; the Council of Trent and Vatican I; the Second Vatican Council and the years which have followed it.

Christian Sacramentality: Roots in Judaism

Since the Christian community had its origins among Jews, efforts to understand the history of Christianity and its development must look to Judaism for the setting within which Christian faith began. A historical survey of Christian sacramental life must learn from the rituals and symbols of Judaism and the central role which these play in the expression and celebration of the faith of the Jewish people.[1]

Jewish faith affirms that God is active in history and present to creation. This faith is expressed in the many rituals and symbols of the Jewish community, which have a twofold focus: the history of the Jewish people and the sacred quality of all life.

The historical focus is apparent in the great importance which the Exodus and covenant have for the Jewish people. The originating event of Jewish faith, the Exodus, formed the Jews into an identifiable community of belief. By this event, God is believed to have acted decisively on behalf of the Jews and chosen them as a people, by delivering them from slavery and the hands of their oppressors. Delivered from their oppressors, they would be led into the land of promise, flowing with milk and honey. At God's initiation, the Jewish people responded by entering into the covenant, a binding agreement between God who promised to be faithful and the people who promised to honor and serve no god but this God, Yahweh. Together, these two realities of Exodus and covenant, which are expressed in Yahweh giving the Torah, the law, and the people observing it faithfully, form the very foundation upon which the Jewish community rests. It is from the perspective of the Exodus and the covenant that the Jewish people remember and tell the story of creation as it is found in the Book of Genesis. For the Jewish mind, the very purpose of creation is the redemption brought about in the Exodus and sealed in the covenant.

God creates to form a people of the covenant. Jewish ritual and symbol are acts of remembrance of the deliverance and the covenant.

Because the God who acts in history is also present to creation, the rituals and symbols of the Jewish community, from the daily benedictions to the benedictions for special occasions, also express the sacred quality of all life. Here it is important to see that the rituals and symbols of Jewish community faith do not focus first on the history of the Jews and then on life's sacredness. Nor is it correct that some rituals and symbols focus exclusively on one dimension while some focus on the other. Rather, they express a twofold reality: God is active in history and present to creation. (The latter is emphasized by the wisdom literature of the Old Testament, like the books of Psalms and Proverbs, while the historical books of the Old Testament, like Joshua and Judges, emphasize Exodus and covenant.)

The Sanctification of Time, Space, and the Passage of Life in Judaism

Jewish ritual is above all a celebration of covenant community and a historical remembrance. Because God is perceived as active in history and present to creation, time, space, and the passage of life are understood to be holy. This sense of the holy is ritualized by Jewish faith. On the other hand, time, space, and life's passage are sanctified, set apart as holy, through ritual precisely because God's presence and activity in them are observed and celebrated. Here again it is essential to recall that all such ritual and symbolic activity is rooted in and refers, more or less explicitly, to the Exodus and covenant as these are expressed in Torah and in faithful observance of it.

THE SANCTIFICATION OF TIME

The remembrance by the Jewish community of the events of its history, primarily as recounted in the Scriptures, is central to its ritual and symbolic life. But the aim is not simply to recall past events and honor God for what has been. In the Jewish understanding, remembering the past is crucial to worship in the present. Acts of worship are done in memory of past events of salvation, so that people can continue to share in those events and benefit from the promises they offer. As a result, Jewish worship looks not simply to the past, but to the present and to the future as well. History is dynamic: not only *has* God acted in the past, but God *is* active and present, and *will be* active and present to the people according to what has been promised. The covenant and law, given long ago, are still binding, as they will always be for the chosen people who strive to be faithful.

This is what is meant by the sanctification of time. The high holy days (Passover, Pentecost, and Tabernacles) and the festivals of Rosh Hashanah (New Year) and Yom Kippur (Day of Atonement) are celebrations of God's creative and saving activity past, present, and to come. One of these, Passover, is perhaps the central symbolic expression of Judaism's faith.

The feast of Passover is the annual commemoration of the most significant event of Jewish community faith, the Exodus. Lengthy preparation precedes Passover, which takes place in the springtime. Though it may have roots in much earlier rites of spring or a spring festival, it is a historical commemoration of God's deeds on behalf of the Jewish people. Central to Passover is the ritual meal which takes place in the home. There are special foods prepared, a special table set, and particular gestures and actions which accompany the meal. Scripture is read and blessing prayers offered, all of which recount the activity of God on behalf of the Jewish people, particularly the events leading up to, including, and following the Exodus.

Much more could be said in description of Passover. Its name stems from the incident leading up to the Exodus in which the angel of death "passed over" the homes of the Jewish people, while slaying the firstborn of their oppressors. The Torah which spells out the responsibilities and obligations of the people of the covenant, gives specific instructions as to how and why Passover is to be observed. In observing Passover and in keeping the weekly Sabbath, which may be said to be like a weekly Passover celebration (in much the same way that Sunday Mass is a weekly celebration of Easter), Jews make their most important expression of faith in the God of the Jewish people as one who is active in history and present to life and all creation, past, present, and to come. No time exceeds God's grasp. Time itself is sanctified, rendered holy, by ritual and the symbolic expression of faith in the God who is at once beyond time, yet active in the history, past, present, and future, of this people.

THE SANCTIFICATION OF SPACE

The importance of the sanctification of space lies in its bringing together historical remembrance and the Jewish sense of God's presence to creation. A number of symbols and rituals are used for the purposes of sanctifying space, of declaring this ground or place holy, of marking this or that spot sacred. There are far too many to describe here, but let us single out one which may be familiar.

The *mezuzah* is found in a variety of forms. Basically a small box or container which is placed on the door of the Jewish home, it contains a small scroll or slip of paper on which are written the words of Scripture recalling the deliverance of the Jewish people from the hands of the Egyptians in the Exodus event. The *mezuzah* causes one to remember God's activity in the history of the chosen people. The Jew reverences the *mezuzah* upon entry into the home, which is marked as a Jewish home precisely through the placing of the *mezuzah* on the door. This space, this environment, is sanctified, marked off as a home of the chosen, God's holy people, by the *mezuzah*. The placing of the *mezuzah* is itself a fulfillment of what is written in the Torah, again illustrating the connection between ritual and faith (Deut. 6:4–9).

What Jews do with the *mezuzah* when the family moves from the home is noteworthy. If the home is sold to another Jewish family, the *mezuzah* remains on the doorpost. Although there may be exceptions to this, the *mezuzah* is taken down from the doorpost if the home is sold to non-Jews. This practice illustrates the Jewish conviction that only those who share the same experience and story, that of the Exodus and covenant, are able to understand and participate in the ritual and symbolic system of Judaism.

Many more examples of the sanctification of space might be cited.[2] It is important above all else to see the role which symbol and ritual play in sanctifying space or environment for those who look to God's activity and presence in their history and the whole of created existence.

THE SANCTIFICATION OF THE PASSAGE OF LIFE

Time's passing is viewed from the perspective shaped by belief in God's action for and in the people. The implications of this are expressed clearly in the rituals by which the Jewish people sanctify the movements and passages in life. These rituals also strengthen their sense of identity as a people, a community of faith.

The religious ritual of *brit milah*, or circumcision, symbolizes the welcoming of the newborn male into the covenant people. Covenant is not a theological abstraction. The covenant is engraved, as it were, upon the flesh of the male Jewish child through the ritual of circumcision. For the Jew the whole ritual of circumcision aims at bestowing a distinct identity upon the child, an identity which is formed by participation in the life of a people set apart through the covenant.

The *bar mitzvah* is the Jewish ritual with which most non-Jews may be familiar. It usually occurs at the age of puberty when the young Jewish male has given sufficient evidence of his intelligence and self-awareness. (In recent years, the *bath mitzvah*, a rite for the coming of age of young women, has gained prominence. However, there is no prescription for this practice in the law.) *Bar mitzvah* is a rite which expresses a conviction that both the young man and the community are persons of the covenant bound to the observance of the law.

Through the Jewish marriage rite the man and the woman continue the lineage of the covenant people. The whole setting of the Jewish marriage ritual is symbolic. Under the wedding canopy the man and woman to be married are viewed as the mythic figures of Adam and Eve, the first parents. Yet in the Jewish mind, even Adam and Eve are seen in terms of the covenant, even Adam and Eve are looked upon as children of Zion. The joy of this new creation (in Adam and Eve) is a foreshadowing of the joy of the messiah's coming (for Jerusalem), a hope which is present in the very hour of the marriage of the bride and the groom. When the messiah comes the joy will echo the joy of this bride and groom. Zion, the bride, and Israel, the groom, stand under the marriage canopy. Though this symbolism may sound odd at first reading, the Christian view of marriage is not unlike this. The whole ritual of Christian marriage, which is likewise symbolic in nature, views the union of man and woman from the perspective of the union between Christ and the church. Just as the Jewish ritual of marriage views the bride and groom as the new Eve and the new Adam (Zion and Israel), so does the Christian ritual of marriage view the bride and groom as the new Eve and the new Adam (church and Christ).

At death or in preparation for death or in memory of the dead, the *kaddish* prayers are said. The *kaddish* prayers are shot through with a sense of loss, longing, desire, hope, and lamentation. These prayers are the last of the major rituals observed in what we have called the sanctification of the passage of life.

A more in-depth treatment of each of the rituals of the passage of life would deepen the understanding of how profound the Jewish sense is of the sacred in all of life.[3]

Concluding Observations

Christian faith and sacramental life are virtually incomprehensible if they are not understood in light of their Jewish background. Jewish faith is focused upon history and the sacredness of life and is ritually expressed in the sanctification of time, space, and the passage of life. Central is the remembrance of the Exodus and covenant, expressed in the observance of the law and the keeping of the Passover. The key notion of memory provides us with entry into the New Testament period because it is historical remembrance, above all else, which Christians retain from Jewish liturgy.

The ritual and symbolic expression of faith in Judaism is found in temple ritual and synagogue worship, as well as domestic ritual. If we have looked here mainly to domestic ritual focused upon the family, it should be noted that temple ritual which centers on priest and sacrifice and synagogue worship which focuses upon word and teaching are also components of Jewish worship which shaped the setting in which Christian faith began.

The New Testament Period

The contours of Christian sacramental life took shape in the New Testament period against a background of enormous diversity and development. There was at this time no universal form of worship. Christian liturgy drew upon current Jewish practices because the first followers of Jesus were Jews. Forms of Jewish worship familiar to the earliest Christians were modified in light of the new faith in Jesus Christ. Practices which were thought to be out of keeping with the meaning and message of Jesus were challenged and revised. Those which were seen to be out of step with the spiritual freedom which was seen to come through faith in Jesus Christ were put aside. What one sees, if an honest look is turned toward the liturgical practice of the New Testament period, is not our present practice or understanding of church and sacrament in miniature but a small movement formed by the spirit of Judaism and its ritual practices, yet groping to give adequate expression to the new faith in Jesus Christ. In passing, it needs to be noted that expressions of faith at this time were influenced also by practices of the Jews of the diaspora (those outside Palestine who were subject to non-Jewish influences) and by some gentile customs.

Centrality of the Cross

It was because Jesus' disciples believed that the crucified one had been raised and continued to live among them that they gathered to worship together and to share a common life. Whereas in Jewish religious expression the Exodus and the covenant provide the root and reference for ritual and communal life, the root and reference for worship in the life of the followers of Jesus was his cross. It is important to note, however, that these need to be seen together, not in opposition to one another. The Exodus is looked at by Jews as an experience of liberation and freedom brought about by God's activity in their history. Likewise, the first followers of Jesus looked to his cross and Resurrection as the promised liberation brought about by God's activity in history through the person of Jesus Christ.

Focus upon the cross did not exclude belief in the Resurrection. But it was primarily the remembrance of the cross of Jesus which is characteristic of early Christian worship. Current biblical studies and interpretation have rediscovered, or recovered, the earliest faith in the Resurrection, which might best be expressed as: The crucified one lives![4]

Desacralization of Worship

Though Christianity retained from Jewish worship the importance of historical remembrance, this emphasis (upon remembrance of Jesus Christ and of his cross) resulted in what may be called *the desacralization of worship*. Slowly and gradually, rather than suddenly and all at once, followers of Jesus began to look less and less to sacred places (such as the temple), sacred times, and sacred persons as central in their worship. Hence the term *desacralization*. For a great variety of reasons, temple worship, circumcision, and sabbath keeping were practiced less and less by the followers of Jesus. The discontinuation of such practices, often without specific religious practices to take their place, resulted in a shift in the understanding of the holy, of how God is present. The meaning of the holy began to change.

Jewish notions of priesthood and sacrifice were profoundly affected by the new faith in Jesus Christ, with important consequences for the ways in which roles and relationships in the new community were viewed. The New Testament calls no one in the community "priest." The term is reserved for Jesus Christ alone. The

New Testament has no place for what may be called priestly ritual. The early Christians had no priesthood. That is to say, there was no particular group set apart from the community for specifically religious activities. Priestly imagery is used only to describe the whole community of people who have been redeemed in Jesus Christ. By their actions in obedience to the gospel they offer a perfect act of sacrifice to God and, as such, are a priestly people.

To desacralize is not to set aside the holy. It is rather to see the meaning of the holy in a different light. This change in understanding may be seen in a threefold movement: from temple sacrifice to table of remembrance; from priest and priesthood to priestly people; and from ritual sacrifice to the sacrifice of obedience to the gospel. Early Christians had no priesthood and no sacrifice other than their remembrance of Jesus and his cross, their sacrifice of obedience to his gospel and the praise of God offered through such obedience. The sacramental life of the early church grew up around these realities, and not around ritual, cult, and priest. As a result, one can refer to this period as one of desacralization, or a period marked by a strong antiritual bias.[5]

The Importance of Word, Narrative, and Thanks

Early Christian worship gave great attention to the proclamation and hearing of the word, to historical remembrance, and to prayers of thanks and blessing. The tradition of priest and sacrificial cult, which prevailed in some currents of Judaism, was set aside. Distinctions between persons, between priest and nonpriest, were understood to be incompatible with the message of Jesus.[6] The community is itself priestly through salvation in Jesus Christ. The attention which the Christians of the New Testament period gave to word, to narrating the story of what God had done in Jesus, and to giving thanks indicates that the primary focus in the worship of the early church was historical and eschatological. Eschatology is the study or understanding of what is to come at the end of time. Christian worship looked to the past from the standpoint of the present with an eye to the future. In the proclamation of the word which tells of God's activity in the past, especially in the life and death of Jesus Christ, the early Christian community expressed its belief that God is also active and present in their assembly at worship, promising them a future yet to come. God's presence in the early church was discerned primarily in history, life, and world. This historical and eschatological understanding is a very different view from what we might call a hierophanic or cosmic view. In this latter understanding, God is understood to exist in a totally other realm, above and beyond our universe, to whom access is made possible through cult and priesthood. But from a historical and eschatological focus the keynotes are word, narrative, and thanks for what God has done in and through our history, in this world, through the person of Jesus Christ who holds out to us a promise of future. Only secondarily, and to a much lesser degree, is early Christian liturgical practice shaped by the hierophanic and cosmic view of worship.

Again, it cannot be stressed strongly enough how important the notion of remembrance is. Acts of Christian worship were and are done in memory of past events of salvation, so that persons may continue to participate in these salvific events and receive the promises they offer. Since the aim of Christian worship is to remember Jesus Christ and God's action in him, especially at the table of the Lord's Supper, the Jewish practice of memorial became the center of Christian liturgy. Memory is the heart of liturgy, but there is a difference between Jewish and Christian memorial. Jewish remembrance is focused upon God's action in their history. Christians remember not only a historical event in which God acted to save them but also God's activity and presence in the *person* of Jesus.

In summary, the New Testament manifests a clear antiritual bias which is indicative of the tendency to desacralize worship during this period. Remembrance, word, narrative, and thanks, none of which are the keynotes of priestly, cultic, sacrificial ritual, are the keynotes of this historical and eschatological view of faith, salvation, and worship. Early Christian worship kept the memory of the cross of the one put to death and raised up, who makes of those who keep his memory and obey his gospel a priestly people, a living sacrifice of praise, who, in life and liturgy become an act of worship to God.

The Patristic Period

The patristic period is that age of church history which followed the time of the New Testament and that of the apostolic fathers (e.g., Ignatius of Antioch, Clement of Rome), those writers who were contemporaneous with or who lived shortly after the New Testament authors. The term *patristic* is related to our word *father*. The patristic period is the one in which lived the great church fathers such as Ambrose (bishop of Milan, d. 397), Augustine (bishop of Hippo Regius, North Africa, d. 430), Cyril of Jerusalem (famous for his *Catechetical Lectures*, one of the chief sources of our present-day *Rite of Christian Initiation of Adults*, d. 386), John Chrysostom ("the golden-tongued" preacher bishop of Constantinople, d. 407), Basil "the Great" of Caesarea (theologian and promoter of the monastic life, d. 379), and Theodore of Mopsuestia (theologian and biblical scholar, d. 428). The term *patristic* is useful, but it should not blind the contemporary Christian to the realization that during this period of the church's history, there were mothers as well as fathers in the faith. When preaching, official teaching, and theologizing are activities which only men are permitted to participate in, and when church life and practice are increasingly influenced by male bias and patriarchy as they were during the patristic period and are in our own day, then names and voices of women, our mothers in faith and mothers of the church, are often overlooked and forgotten. Contemporary theologians, men as well as women, have attempted to rediscover the legacy of these women in the New Testament period and in early church history.[7]

During this period, the keynotes for understanding the development of Christian sacramental life are *adaptation* and *resacralization*. This is especially true when it comes to understanding ministry or service in the church. If the New Testament period was marked by a tendency toward desacralization, with a strong antiritual bias and an emphasis upon the *priestly people* saved in Jesus Christ, in the patristic period there was a return of *cult and priest* with a reemergence of awe and reverential fear in the face of what came to be viewed as *sacred places, sacred times, and sacred persons.*

Adaptation

As Christian faith spread beyond the immediate surroundings in which Jesus of Nazareth lived, the followers of Jesus found themselves faced with the task of adapting Christian faith to new and varied cultures. In any age, if religious faith is to be effective, it must adapt to meet the needs of particular persons and groups in different cultural settings.[8] We witnessed this type of adaptation recently in the reformed liturgy following Vatican II, which recognized the need to celebrate the sacraments in the languages of local peoples. Prior to Vatican II, the universal language of the church at liturgy was Latin. Though there were rare exceptions, all peoples throughout the world celebrated in the same tongue. Some would prefer still to have the sacraments celebrated in Latin and argue that the universal language binds people together in such a way that one could walk into a Catholic church in Paris, Rome, Rio, or Richmond and feel "at home" there. The problem with this line of thinking is that what actually "binds" people together, what makes them "feel at home," is a shared ignorance and confusion about what is actually being celebrated. The importance of word in sacramental celebration pointed out in the documents of Vatican II makes it clear that liturgy and sacrament must undergo constant adaptation so as to meet the needs and urgencies of particular communities in diverse cultural settings.

An example of this cultural adaptation of liturgy may be seen in the role which the *basilica* came to play in Christian worship after Emperor Constantine legalized Christianity through the Edict of Milan (313), or the Edict of Toleration. Earlier, Christian worship was held in domestic settings because Christians were not free to gather in public places for their worship. The increased number of Christians in the church of free Rome made it necessary to move to a larger meeting place. The basilica was not at first understood as a sacred place, but a large meeting place. In other words, Christians first met there for worship solely because it was a place large enough to accommodate their growing numbers. The dignity of the basilica derived from the dignity of God's people, who met and worshiped there. Only later did the basilica come to be understood as a sacred place.

Another example of cultural adaptation may be seen in the great variety of eucharistic prayers which highlight different understandings of Christ and his mysteries. The eucharistic prayer is the great prayer of thanksgiving within the Mass, that part of the Mass which forms the real heart and soul of Christian worship. It is the prayer spoken aloud by the presider (priest), in which God the Creator is thanked, the Spirit is invoked, Christ's passion, death, and rising remembered, and God's praise and glory proclaimed for what has been given us in Jesus Christ. Basil of Caesarea's prayer highlights the Incarnation, by which the Word of God became flesh in Jesus Christ. Hippolytus's (d. 236) gives great attention to the descent of Christ into hell. The Roman Canon emphasizes the sacrificial element of Christ's death. The point is not to question which is right or wrong, true or false. Rather, the variety of eucharistic prayers illustrates the different ways in which the church in diverse communities in different cultural settings actively remembered Christ. This cultural adaptation marks the development of the sacramental life of the church and the growth of Christian faith throughout the first millennium and beyond.

Resacralization

Within this process of cultural adaptation one dominant tendency which had great influence upon later sacramental life and theology was that of resacralization. With the granting of state recognition to the Christian faith its practice was influenced by practices prevalent in Roman culture. Christian worship came to be viewed primarily in terms of sacrifice, and it came to be influenced by the mind-set and language of both *temple worship* and the *imperial court*. Christian celebrations took on some of the characteristics of pagan feasts and at times replaced them. Especially in northern European countries, Christian churches were built upon the site of pagan temples. At times these churches were built through a process of restructuring and transforming an already existing pagan temple. At other times pagan structures were completely demolished, and Christian ones put in their place. The point is that erecting sacred shrines or churches on pagan holy places indicated a change in direction from that of the New Testament period which looked primarily to the community of faith in Jesus Christ as holy, and any ground on which they stood as sacred. Erecting Christian churches on sites of pagan holy places gives indication of this tendency of resacralization—a tendency which is quite different from the de-sacralization or antiritual bias of the New Testament period.

Part of this tendency of resacralization was to emphasize *the priestly character of the bishop.* This then introduced distinctions in the body of believers, distinctions which are not well supported by the message of Jesus and the gospel, and which resulted in an emphasis upon hierarchy over ministry or service.

In time the church was no longer viewed as a large meeting place made holy by virtue of Christians' dignity as the People of God, but as a sacred place because the sacred activity of offering sacrifice by the bishop-priest took place there.

What is important to note in all of these developments is that Christian liturgy changes as a result of cultural influences upon it. During this period of cultural adaptation the sacramental initiation process (through baptism, confirmation, and Eucharist) and the ritual of Christian burial came to fulfill the function of social life passage in some countries. No longer were Christians small gatherings of people who were going against dominant cultural currents and who were committed to a faith which transformed their way of living. No longer was Christian initiation a radical renunciation of one way of life and a mature and responsible embrace of another. As persons were born into a culture which became increasingly "christianized," the church took on the role of nourishing and protecting faith from birth to death and of providing religious ceremonies for all family and civic occasions. The problem here is that it was often the case that

Christian faith became virtually indistinguishable from common-place social behavior, and Christian ritual ran the risk of providing a sense of social cohesion based more upon social customs than anything particularly Christian.

ADAPTATION AND RESACRALIZATION: FOR BETTER OR WORSE?

The question is not whether such cultural adaptation of liturgy was valid, but whether, in such adaptation of Christian faith and worship, something of the original essence of faith in Jesus Christ was lost. Due to the increased numbers of Christians in free Rome, a larger worship space became necessary. But it must be asked whether the practices of the Roman court system, with its hierarchical roles and persons of high distinction, did not influence the style of Christian worship in the basilica to the point that it resulted in a type of liturgy that was in conflict with the message of Jesus, which does not allow for distinction of persons based upon rank (Gal. 3:27–28).

The influence of the Roman court and of temple worship has had a lasting impact on Christian liturgy, which is felt even to this day. One must face seriously the question: In what ways does contemporary liturgy, in mirroring the hierarchical structure of the Roman court, fail to serve the community of equal servants and disciples who gather in memory of the one who would not allow for distinction of persons based upon rank? Ultimately the question is whether some cultural adaptations of Christian faith, for example, adaptation to the models of power as exercised in the Roman imperial court, damage the transmission of the message of Jesus Christ. Further, how can such practice be integrated into a form of worship that is essentially a community's act of remembrance of one who stood with the poor and wounded, marginal and forgotten people, those without rank, prestige, or influence?

Resacralization and a strong emphasis on hierarchy may lead one to conclude that the patristic period departed from an essential message of the gospel. Whatever judgment one may make, the church during this period was marked by a deep symbolic sensitivity, which stands in striking contrast to the naive understanding of symbol which emerged in later currents of thought and practice in Western Christianity. The church fathers each have their own way of describing sacrament but, for the most part, it may be said that they envision sacrament as a real participation in the mystery of Christ. The focus is upon a real sharing in the cross and Resurrection of Jesus Christ and a changed way of life because of this participation. Symbol, ikon, and other related terms describe realities which allow Christ's mysteries to be present. This is not mere representation. The sacrament does not "stand for" something else which is "more real." Nor is the sacrament simply an instrument for the communication of grace.

During this period a sacrament was understood in a broad sense, broader than the sevenfold ritual system as it later emerged. Sacrament is umbrellalike and covers such rich realities as the various feasts of the Christian year, reading and proclaiming the gospel, prayers of blessing, Christ, the church, ritual acts, and the lives of Christian people obedient to the gospel.

Sacramental rituals are not the only symbols of God's presence in world, life, history, and church. In the patristic period the Sacred Scriptures and images of God's presence, such as an ikon, were also included. But sacramental activity, especially that of the eucharistic liturgy, or Mass, is distinguished from all these in that it is the gathering of the Body of Christ and the bringing together of all the other symbols through which the church expresses and participates in the mystery of Christ whose Body the church has become.

Other currents of thought and practice within the patristic period give evidence of a loss of symbolic sensitivity, a loss which comes to characterize much of later Western Christian thought. In some patristic writers and practices, we see a tendency to view symbol not only as a reality which represents and invites to real participation and sharing with a higher reality, but also as a reality which to some degree veils the higher and more perfect reality which it communicates. An example of these currents would lie in the overdramatization of Christian liturgy and an emphasis upon the concrete objects, actions, gestures, or words themselves instead of the community's use of these. For example, focus is placed upon the bread rather than the breaking of bread, upon the water, rather than the washing with water, and upon the oil, rather than the anointing with oil. Overdramatization may be seen in the way in which the "words of consecration" are often said slowly, audibly, reverently, while what precedes and follows is said and done in such haste and with so little apparent interest that the end product is a "twenty-minute Mass," the only point of which appears to be the consecration of the bread and wine.

The High Middle Ages

In the first chapter we turned attention briefly to the thirteenth century and the hierarchical world view which was characteristic of that time. This world view, which began to take root much earlier than the Middle Ages, must be seen as both related to the nature and function of symbol and contributing toward the gradual loss of that symbolic sensitivity which was characteristic of earlier periods. Medieval Western thought lost touch with what might be called symbolic perception.

In much of the thought and practice of the Middle Ages the symbol was reduced to the role of an instrument, that which brings something else about. As a result, the symbol became strongly distinguished from reality. In bringing something about it was referred to as a *cause of grace.* That is to say, symbol and reality came to be viewed as two very different things. The symbol, or sign, as it was now referred to, was reduced to an instrumental function in the face of the *reality signified.* The reality signified was seen to be the *really real.* In this view the sign, such as bread or water, existing as it does in the material order of being, which was understood to be lower or less perfect in being, points to or communicates a higher, more perfect reality. The connection was lost: the symbol and the symbolized, the sign and the signified, which need to be distinguished, were now not simply distinguished but separated one from the other. Gone was the sense in which symbols are themselves realities which represent and invite sharing and are themselves a participation in Christ's mysteries. Concrete things, actions, gestures, words came to be understood as lesser realities which veil the mystery of the *really real,* which was understood to exist in the higher order of the immaterial. Sacraments came to be understood as visible signs which serve as instruments of invisible grace.

Effects on Lay People

Together with this strong separation between sign and reality, the Middle Ages, again due in large measure to the hierarchical world view, had a view of church which gave enormous emphasis to institutional factors and to a hierarchical model of church life and ministry, or service in the church.

In church life and practice lay persons were reduced to passivity. Liturgical life of lay persons became a matter of looking on. Their role was to receive sacraments. The laity had become spectators. There was great accent on the visual in an effort to bring about awe of and devotion to the sacraments. The actions, gestures, things, and words which once were viewed as disclosures or manifestations of God's presence were now explained as material signs which are an obscure representation, indeed a veiling, of a higher reality. The sacramental rituals came to be seen as instruments and reminders which aroused devotion and feeling for something beyond, rather than symbolic acts which in themselves participate in the love and presence of Christ. In this view, sacraments were a type of illustration of a reality which was looked upon as totally obscure. This obscure reality, which was understood to be the *really real*, was known only by faith, a type of faith which contradicted what was perceived by the senses. The faithful were told to believe not in what their senses perceived, for that was a representation or illustration which veiled and clouded even more the obscure reality which only the eyes of faith could see. Believers were warned to affirm what authority prescribed. As a result, shaky faith and doubt were met not with catechesis, or teaching, based upon the persuasiveness of the symbols which disclosed Christ's presence in themselves. Rather, questions and doubts were often responded to with stories of miracles which were intended to convince on the basis of divine intervention and sacred power. To this mind, the bread and wine of the Eucharist become the Body and Blood of Christ because Christ said they would, and through God's power invested in the priest, by means of which God intervenes in the ordinary course of human affairs.

Power and Authority Replace Quality of Symbol

Even in the thought of Thomas Aquinas, who avoids many of the pitfalls of others attempting to understand and explain sacrament in the Middle Ages, sacraments are understood in terms of divine power. He argues for Christ's presence in sacraments largely in terms of divine power invested in the priest through ordination. Whatever may be argued in favor of Aquinas's understanding of sacrament, it must be pointed out that his focus is on divine and priestly power to such an extent that he does not give much attention to an adequate explanation of the nature and function of symbol. He understood Christ's presence to be brought about exclusively by power and authority. In practice, if not in theory, this meant that the nature of the things—such as bread, oil, and water—used in sacramental celebration disclosed or manifested very little. They only served to visualize or illustrate what one already believed on the basis of authority. Further, the quality of the sign was not recognized as important. The question in the Middle Ages was not whether this or that concrete object, gesture, act, or word of itself seemed suited to disclose God's presence. Only authority guaranteed sacramental presence, which was thought to be given regardless of the quality of sign. So, for example, whether the waters of baptism were sprinkled, dabbed, lavishly poured, or set in a pool for dunking did not matter. What mattered was the guarantee that through water and words one's sins were forgiven. How so? Not so much, in this view, by virtue of Christ's presence being effectively communicated through a given symbol, but because Christ said so, and the priest had the power to do it.

The effects of this mentality are still felt today. Liturgy that is poorly planned, bread that looks, tastes, smells, and feels like anything but bread, eucharistic prayers rushed through in a matter of minutes, all give indication of a mind which views the separation of symbol and reality as the status quo. The symbols themselves don't really matter. In the final analysis, the liturgical activity is not seen to bring about presence; presence depends solely and exclusively on the correct exercise of the power of the ordained.

Reification

With this strong separation between sign and reality, and with the heavy emphasis upon the hierarchical and institutional elements of the church and on priestly power, sacraments went through a process of *reification*, a term deriving from the Latin word for *thing*.

Though not all medieval theologians contributed to this process of reification (Thomas Aquinas certainly stands against it to some degree), the sacraments came to be viewed as things, or objects, separated from their own deepest meanings. In themselves, these things only served to point to reality, which was known only by faith. They were objects which in themselves veiled the real, that to which faith looked in looking beyond them.

This reification, or objectification, took place on another level as well. The sacraments were taken out of the hands of the believing community, as is clear in the example of withholding the cup from lay persons. Sometime prior to the twelfth and thirteenth centuries the practice of drinking from the cup by all in the assembly fell into disfavor. By the high Middle Ages the practice of withholding the chalice from the laity was firmly established. With the focus on the hierarchy and the church as primarily an institution, sacraments became less and less the corporate activity of a community, and more and more the act of one of its members, in whose presence the majority looked on. Sacraments became somebody else's business— "out there," "up there." They came to be seen as objects out of reach, like the chalice, things in the face of which the vast majority understood themselves to be unworthy. Reification has its counterparts even in contemporary practice. Many view sacraments as things, not communal activities. The church is viewed as an "it" or a thing, not as a "we." And the cup of wine given for all is still up there, out there, a thing seen but not touched or tasted in any number of Catholic parish settings.

The deep symbolic sensitivity of the patristic period gave way to a view in the Middle Ages which looked upon things or words as indications or representations of a higher truth or more perfect reality. Concrete gestures, actions, things, and words were separated from their deepest meanings. This is radically different from a sacramental view and principle, one marked by deep symbolic sensitivity and perception, which allows and invites us to look to the symbols in and of themselves for a disclosure, manifestation, and promise of the truth present in them.[9]

The Reformation

The Reformation took place gradually, its roots deeper than the story of Luther's nailing of the ninety-five theses on the cathedral door (1517). Its motivations are related to what we have said about the Middle Ages. Few today would dispute that the church was in need of reform. The church of the later Middle Ages began to look less and less like a community of service and discipleship. Martin Luther, and those who followed him, challenged the church of their day to return to the spirit and practice of the gospel and to reform its scandalous practices, especially those abuses in the realm of sacramental life. No one could have foreseen or imagined the impact that challenge would have.

It is nearly impossible to trace the essential contours of the Reformation in these few pages, and difficult enough to spell out the contribution of the Reformation to the history of the sacramental life of the church. Strange as it may seem to Roman Catholic readers, the Protestant Reformation did make a contribution to the sacramental life of the church, even if its effects were not recognized until much later.

Roman Catholic grade schoolers once learned that Protestants ("they") don't believe in the sacraments. This is one of many such statements made in Catholic grade school classrooms that need to be nuanced. Most mainline Protestant churches do have a liturgical life. Although the different churches vary on the importance they attach to sacrament, most Protestant churches do have sacramental celebrations.

Martin Luther accepted sacraments as vital to Christian life. But, for Luther, faith has priority over all else. That does not mean that the sacraments are set aside. It does mean that, for Luther, sacraments need to be viewed within the context of faith, not power and authority—faith in God's Word, Jesus Christ, above all else.

In his effort to return to the spirit of the gospel and to the practices of the earliest church, Luther placed strong emphasis upon the word of God in Scripture. Since Scripture was the norm for him, everything fell under its judgment. In his reading and interpretation of Scripture Luther was not slow to see that the only two sacraments which are clearly supported by the New Testament are baptism and Eucharist. Whatever basis for the development of the other sacraments one may care to suggest that the New Testament provides, the only ones which are clearly based in the New Testament are baptism and Eucharist. Hence these two sacraments had priority over the others in the mind of Luther and, he argued, should have priority in the sacramental life of the church.

Luther saw a model for Christian life in the life of the early Christian community. In Luther's view, many church practices of his day were not well supported by Scripture. In so many ways church life and structure seemed to go against the message of Jesus. He argued against mandatory celibacy for clergy and against the church's preoccupation with its own hierarchical and institutional structures. He insisted on the priesthood of all believers as essential to Christian faith. Rather than viewing priest and Eucharist in terms of sacrifice, Luther maintained that the sacrifice had been offered once for all by Jesus. Those saved by his sacrifice of obedience unto death are a priestly people whose only sacrifice is obedience to the gospel and worship of God.

The contribution of Luther's reform to the development of sacramental life in the church is contained in three points: the importance of the word, the priesthood of all believers, and the centrality of the assembly.

Importance of the Word

Worship in the later Middle Ages gave little place to the proclamation and hearing of the word in Scripture. Since the sacraments themselves were seen as a display of divine power and authority invested in the priest, the liturgical life of the church revolved around them. Because the language of the church and of Scripture was Latin, both were off limits to the ordinary Christian, who more often than not could not read, speak, or write Latin. Part of Luther's contribution was to place the Scriptures in the hands of the people in their own language so that it became a foundation in Christian life and worship and a formative influence in both. From this perspective everything is judged by the word of God, instead of by the authoritative voice of the priest. As a result, Christian worship became less focused upon cult and the sacred acts of the priest, and more upon proclamation, narrative, and commemoration, which are all expressions of the word.

Priesthood of All Believers

Our earlier treatment of sacrament in the Middle Ages drew attention to the view of the sacraments as things or objects which were dispensed by hierarchs and priests, and received by lay persons. Liturgy and sacrament were someone else's business. The laity assisted and looked at what was essentially the act of the priest. With Luther's rediscovery of the fundamental New Testament theme of the priesthood of all believers, it became possible for all baptized Christians, not just priests, monks, and nuns, to understand themselves as mature and responsible persons entrusted with, and empowered by, the word and work of Jesus Christ.

The Centrality of the Assembly

What followed from Luther's rediscovery of the theme of the priesthood of all believers was that the church's worship needed to take account of the priestly people called in baptism and enlightened by grace and Spirit. In Luther's view of worship, what is central is not the priest, or ritual sacrifice, but all the baptized who assemble in memory of the one whose word compels them to believe and obey, and whose coming is anticipated in the community's act of breaking bread and sharing the cup.

By no means can this be understood as a survey of the Reformation's contribution to sacramental life. In selecting the three points of word, priestly people, and assembly which were crucial in the life and theology of Martin Luther, we have glimpsed elements which have been foundational in Protestant worship and liturgy. Only centuries later have these elements come to be recognized in Roman Catholic sacramental life and theology as crucial for a proper understanding of sacrament.

For many Catholic sacramental theologians and liturgists, the problem remains that Luther did not sufficiently allow these important factors to influence his understanding of the sacraments. With his focus upon the absolute priority of the word and of faith, Luther showed a still greater disregard for symbols and deep symbolic sensitivity than did some in the Middle Ages, and in other early periods. Also his emphasis upon the priesthood of all believers at times gives indication of a hazy theology of ministry. Even if one agrees that all the baptized share in the priesthood of Jesus Christ, and therefore are called to ministry by virtue of their baptism, there still remains the need to recognize that gifts and calls to service differ, and that some ministries in the church cannot be exercised at random.

The Council of Trent and Vatican I

Two key events, the Council of Trent in the mid-sixteenth century, and the First Vatican Council in the latter part of the nineteenth, fall between the period of the Reformation and the contemporary post–Vatican II era.

The Council of Trent was in large part a response to the events of the Reformation. The statements and the documents of the council need to be looked at with new eyes, so that the council's views may be seen on their own terms, and not through the eyes of later interpreters who may not have provided an accurate or authentic presentation of Trent.

Concerning the sacraments, Trent was concerned to correct certain abuses brought to light during the Reformation, especially practices pertaining to penance and the celebration of Mass. But Trent's approach to sacrament was mainly legalistic and hierarchical. During this council the sevenfold sacramental system was clearly defined. Other definitions with which many Roman Catholics are familiar resulted from Trent. Whatever may have been its positive contributions, Trent did not respond fully to the challenges posed by the Reformation. The council in fact tended to confirm and reinforce the tendencies of the Middle Ages which had been challenged and criticized by the Reformation. It reasserted claims previously made on the basis of divine and priestly power and authority, and attempted to strengthen church life and practice by reasserting the value of doctrines and practices which, for a variety of good reasons, had been called into question by the Reformers. Rather than taking the Reformation as challenge and opportunity to renew and update the doctrines and practices of the Catholic church, Trent tended to defend the legitimacy of precisely those factors which had contributed to the loss of its rooting in the principles and practices of the gospel and the early church.

The First Vatican Council met to address another series of problems. But here again the approach was legalistic and authoritarian. It reaffirmed and reasserted what it thought to be the belief and practice of the church throughout its history. It confirmed the direction of Trent in its juridical approach to the sacraments. The hierarchical and power based model of church triumphed in the council's acceptance of the notion of papal infallibility.

These two councils shaped the texture of Roman Catholic life and sacramental practice for decades to come. Church and sacraments came to be viewed from the perspective of power and authority. Both came through ordination and incorporation into the hierarchy. Grace and sacraments were the priest's domain. The majority of the Body of Christ, the church, came to be viewed as passive recipients; sacrament as means or instrument of grace, and an object of devotion rather than as an act. The church came to be seen as a "they," not a "we" and a way of life. The sentiment still lingers. The picture is not entirely bleak however, for Trent and Vatican I made significant contributions to the development of the sacramental life of the church.

The major contributions of these councils may be stated briefly. First, the Council of Trent and Vatican I provided a strong sense of unity and universality. The church was thought to be always and everywhere the same in what was believed and practiced. Second, they provided a strong sense of coherence and cohesion. Catholics were recognizable to one another and to those outside the church by what they believed and what they practiced. There was little room for diversity, individual interpretation, or local adaptations. Finally, by stressing power and authority, the councils affirmed that God's grace was guaranteed to be available in the sacraments. In a world in which very little was thought to be reliable, at least one could be guaranteed grace, from this perspective.

The Second Vatican Council

In the first chapter Vatican II was the orienting event for a contemporary understanding of sacraments and Christian living. It may be useful here to spell out some of its most significant contributions to the historical development of the sacramental life of the church.

First, with the renewed understanding of the church as the People of God, Vatican II opened the way for a more participatory role for the whole church in sacramental life and worship. This is seen, for example, in the translation of sacramental rites into the language of local peoples, and in the attention which Vatican II gave to the local customs of a people. Ministries or acts of service for the church which prior to this point had been open only to clerics are now exercised by the nonordained. This is also a result of understanding the church as the People of God.

Second, the council recognized the presence of Christ not only in the sacramental rituals of the liturgy, but in the presider (priest), assembly, and the word. The rituals and priest had for many centuries been the focus in thought about and practice of sacramental life. But attention to the word and to the assembly as focal points for the manifold presence of Christ result in a different vision of liturgy and sacrament. The primary symbol in any liturgical activity is the assembly which God calls and commands by the word proclaimed and heard in the church's liturgy.

Third, the council also gave evidence of a deep concern with the way in which symbols express and communicate meaning in sacramental celebration. For example, the bread used in the Eucharist, in accord with the spirit of directives following the council, should look, taste, smell, and feel like bread.[10] Also the oil used in anointing may vary according to culture and according to what may be available given various cultural differences. That is to say, an oil readily available in one culture may be unavailable in another. Consequently, different cultures may anoint with different kinds of oil so that what local peoples recognize as the symbol of oil with its particular healing and soothing qualities may symbolize the healing power of Christ's presence in and through the church.[11]

Fourth, the council held out a nuanced vision of church and world, heaven and earth, the eternal and temporal. The radical separation and opposition between these was dealt a fatal blow in the church's definition of itself as sacrament not only *to* the world but *in* the world. As a result sacraments do not belong simply to the domain of the churchly. Sacraments are not primarily to be understood as a participation in the eternal and an anticipation of the heavenly. Rather, sacraments are seen as communal acts through which the church receives and expresses its call and commitment as the Body of Christ through grace and Spirit. As Body of Christ the church becomes a corporate sign and witness in and to the world. What follows then is a closer connection between liturgy and life, sacrament and Christian living.

Finally, in the *Constitution on the Sacred Liturgy* (nos. 47–58) and in the *Rite of Christian Initiation of Adults*, which resulted from the council's directive to reform and renew the practice of Christian initiation, the council provided the framework for recovering the central importance of baptism and Eucharist in Christian sacramental life. Both envision the Eucharist as source and summit of Christian life. A contemporary view of sacramental life looks to font and table, baptism and Eucharist, as the cornerstones upon which Christian life is built. In baptism one is welcomed into a covenant community and a way of life based upon the covenant. In the Eucharist one participates in a communal act whose hallmarks are communion and justice, centered in the liberating word and work of Jesus Christ.

Contemporary liturgy has been shaped by all of these factors and more. Where good sacramental celebration occurs today, it is largely due to the efforts of Vatican II and those who have accepted its challenge to be sacrament in and to the world, and so to more effectively meet the needs and urgent demands of people in today's world. The task is one of ongoing reform and renewal. The fruits of such reform and renewal may not be born for generations. The careful reader will have noted that the contributions of the Second Vatican Council to the history of sacramental life, which have been cited, bear striking similarity to the themes which shaped the life and theology of Martin Luther. Be it noted, however, that the council gave evidence of a much greater appreciation of symbol and sacrament than did Luther.

Contemporary sacramental life and theology, shaped by a renewed Christology, ecclesiology, and anthropology, must look to the wisdom of the Second Vatican Council and to the gospel of Jesus Christ above all else for the principles and spirit which will shape the ongoing renewal and reform of the sacramental life of the church, as we move into a future age marked by types and degrees of pluriformity and diversity without precedent in the history of church and world.

Notes

1. The *Jewish people*, or *Jews*, is the term used to describe the people who at various times in their history may be more properly referred to as Hebrews, Israel, Israelites. The term *Jews* or *Jewish people* is not employed to overlook this difference, but simply to avoid possible confusion of terms.

2. See Richard Siegel, Michael Strassfeld, and Sharon Strassfeld, *The First Jewish Catalog* (Philadelphia: Jewish Publication Society of America, 1973).

3. Again, a useful tool for further investigation of this point is *The First Jewish Catalog.*

4. The christological works of Edward Schillebeeckx are particularly helpful on this point. See, for example, *Jesus: An Experiment in Christology* (New York: Seabury Press, 1979), p. 399ff.

5. For a fuller treatment of this notion of desacralization, see David N. Power, *Unsearchable Riches: The Symbolic Nature of Liturgy* (New York: Pueblo Publishing Co., 1984), p. 35ff.

6. See the fine analysis of the early Christian church as a community of coequal disciples in Elisabeth Schüssler Fiorenza, *In Memory of Her* (New York: Crossroad Publishing Co., 1983).

7. For the finest example of the effort to recover the significance of women during the period of Christian origins, see Schüssler Fiorenza, *In Memory of Her.*

8. For a further treatment of this point, see Anscar Chupungco, *Cultural Adaptation of the Liturgy* (New York: Paulist Press, 1982).

9. Power, *Unsearchable Riches*, p. 56.

10. The General Instruction of the Roman Missal, no. 283.

11. See the apostolic constitution on the sacrament of the anointing of the sick, in *Documents on the Liturgy, 1963–1979* (Collegeville, MN: Liturgical Press, 1982), p. 1051ff.

4

Christian Initiation

In this chapter, we begin to look at the seven sacraments of Roman Catholicism with the rite of initiation itself. The rite of initiation is highlighted for two reasons. First, it gives us the opportunity to examine a concrete example of one of the great achievements of the Second Vatican Council, the renewal and reform of the sacramental rites of the church, not only to see what it says about baptism and confirmation but also to make note of the ethical horizon expressed in the rite.

Second, this rite is examined in detail because of its monumental significance in the life of the church. The rite is a masterpiece because of the way it depicts the sacraments of initiation; even more, its importance lies in the understanding of church which it expresses. Indeed some maintain that, when the final page of the history of the liturgical renewal brought about by Vatican II is written, the *Rite of Christian Initiation of Adults*[1] will be portrayed as its most significant contribution to sacramental life and liturgy.[2] For these reasons the vision of church and sacrament found in the *RCIA* command attention. If the church is to meet the needs and demands of the age as it moves into the third millennium of Christian history, then a liturgical and sacramental life more in step with the *RCIA* is required, not simply desired.

Our analysis in this chapter will follow four steps: first, to look at the meaning of the term *initiation*; second, to examine the *RCIA* as a model for Christian initiation and for what it says about the nature of initiation; third, to point out some of the practical problems which arise as a result of using the *RCIA* as a model of initiation, especially the question of the baptism of infants and children; fourth, to note briefly some of the implications of the sacraments of initiation for Christian living.

62

The Meaning of Initiation

If the *RCIA* is used as a model for understanding Christian initiation, then baptism, confirmation, and Eucharist may all be referred to as sacraments of initiation. Since the Eucharist will be treated in the following chapter, the focus here is upon baptism and confirmation.

The term *baptism* brings to mind a whole array of related words and images: white christening gowns, godparents, lighted candles, crying babies, and the sprinkling of water are but a few. Every once in a great while the image of the baptism of an adult may break through.

As a schoolboy I can remember one afternoon when I visited my parish church and barged in on a ceremony of adult baptism. I was awe-struck because I had never seen such a thing, though I knew that sometimes people "finally saw the light and came over to Catholicism." "What took her so long to convert?" was my question. When one grows up in a church which nurtures faith from cradle to grave, such sentiments come naturally.

All the above images and feelings reflect an understanding which is quite different from the meaning of initiation found in the *RCIA*. The term *initiation* is not immediately associated with church and sacraments in the minds of most Roman Catholics—even though the *RCIA* was released in 1972—but with entrance or indoctrination into some club or organization, perhaps a college sorority or the Elks.

In a Christian context, however, the term *initiation* refers to the activities, processes, steps, and stages which one participates in to become a member of the Christian community. It refers to the activities, both liturgical and sacramental, by which one is incorporated into the life of the church. Initiation is not a primarily private, personal affair. It refers to a *process*, not an instantaneous moment. Through the rite of Christian initiation one becomes a vital participant in a community of shared faith, shared vision, and shared life inspired by the life, death and Resurrection of Jesus Christ.

Initiation as it is envisioned in the *RCIA* is quite different from the baptism of adults as I experienced it as a schoolboy. It is quite different, too, from the practice of "receiving converts into the church" which occurred in the days before Vatican II and which required little more than the memorization of the Baltimore Catechism,[3] a few visits to the rectory parlor, and a sprinkle of water in the back of the church on a weekday afternoon. In the understanding of initiation expressed in the *RCIA* the community is responsible for the initiation of new members because it is the church community as Body of Christ into which the convert is initiated. She or he joins in the mission of a community of faith which attempts to become a corporate sign and witness to the world and in the world.

Step by Step:
An Examination of the RCIA

The *Rite of Christian Initiation of Adults* was released in January 1972 by the Sacred Congregation for Divine Worship. It emerged as a result of a mandate given at the Second Vatican Council, which called for the revision of the rite of initiation in use at the time. The council also directed that the catechumenate, or period of instruction, should be recovered and restored as a vital element of the process of initiation within a living and vibrant community of Christian faith and practice.

The *RCIA* includes the full rite of adult initiation, a simple form of the same rite for extraordinary circumstances such as illness, and a brief form for use in danger of death. Three further concerns are accounted for: first, instructions are provided for the confirmation and first Eucharist of adults who were baptized as infants or children, but who were not catechized, or instructed, later; second, rites are provided for children who were not baptized as infants; third, rites are provided for the admission into full communion, or membership, of those who have already been baptized in a Christian church other than Roman Catholic.

The General Instruction to all of these reformed rites of initiation makes it clear that the chief ritual is that of the full initiation of adults. It is for this reason that it is looked at as both a *model and norm for all Christian initiation.*[4] All other rites of initiation are to find their proper place by way of reference to this foremost rite. This is made especially clear since various details of the other rites regularly appeal back to the full rite of adult initiation as the governing pattern for them all. As a consequence, the rationale and principles which lie at the base of the full rite of initiation of adults are to influence all other practices of Christian initiation. In brief, it is the model of Christian initiation which a contemporary treatment of baptism and confirmation as sacraments of initiation must take into account.

True as it is to the richness of the theological, liturgical, and sacramental tradition, the *RCIA* deserves a thorough examination with an eye to the various steps and stages which form the process of initiation—if initiation into a community of shared life, shared vision, shared faith and values is taken seriously.

Precatechumenate

The period of precatechumenate is more properly understood as a prestage. Precatechumenate is a time of initial contact and evangelization, or spreading the gospel. Attracted by the life and practice of a community, an interested person inquires about the community and the possibilities of entry. The members of the community evangelize, not by handing out leaflets on street corners, or by preaching at the entrances of shopping malls, but by offering witness to the message of Jesus Christ and his gospel in their everyday life and in their worship.

Catechumenate

According to the spirit and letter of the *RCIA*, the period of catechumenate—where Christian initiation actually begins—should be of considerable duration. There is some dispute about what considerable duration means. Some would insist on a period of two years; others, that the catechumenate can be moved through more quickly by some people than by others. Interpretation of what considerable duration means should be flexible enough to allow for adaptation to local and particular needs. It should be made clear, however, that the catechumenate is a process which should not be passed over or rushed through quickly in the name of practicality or efficiency.

If the keynote of the period of precatechumenate is *initial contact*, then the keynote of the stage of catechumenate is clearly that of *conversion*. This is a process, not a miraculous moment. It occurs within a vital community of faith, not in a rectory parlor. The catechumenate is a period of learning and of growing in the consciousness of Christ and his mysteries. But such learning and growth do not take place primarily through the teaching of doctrine or through other instructional media. The kind of catechesis envisioned by the *RCIA* is primarily *experiential* and only secondarily instructional.

The process called conversion takes place in three ways: first, through sharing *the life and vision of the community*; second, by becoming familiar with the *teaching of the community*, particularly regarding Scripture and moral life in the church; third, by sharing in the *prayer* and, to a degree, in the *liturgy of the community*.

From this it should be clear that the catechumenate, and the conversion which it aims to bring about, takes place gradually over a considerable period of time, rather than all at once.

Purification and Enlightenment

If the keynote for precatechumenate is initial contact, and the keynote for catechumenate is conversion, then *intensification* is the hallmark of the period of purification and enlightenment. This stage of the initiation rite is geared to an intensification of the dynamics of conversion set in motion through participation in the catechumenate. This stage begins on the first Sunday of Lent. Having spent a considerable period of time sharing the life, vision, teaching, and prayer of the community, the catechumens enter the period of purification and enlightenment through a ceremony of *election* which takes place during the eucharistic liturgy of the first Sunday of Lent. Here, to "elect" means to choose. The catechumens choose to continue and intensify their preparation for entry into full membership in the Body of Christ, the church. They publicly, before the assembly at worship, make known their intention to prepare more intensely for the sacraments of initiation, baptism, confirmation, and Eucharist, to be received during the Easter Vigil. The assembly chooses or elects to receive these catechumens into the life of the church, and promises to support them by praying for and with them during their final period of preparation for celebrating the sacraments of initiation.

The intensification of the process of conversion occurs through a concentrated focus on the themes of the gospels for the third, fourth, and fifth Sundays of Lent. These gospels communicate, in one way or another, the themes of *living water* (the story of the Samaritan woman in John 4), *light* (the cure of the man born blind in John 9), and *life* (the raising of Lazarus in John 11). Hence the name of this stage of the rite of initiation: purification and enlightenment. The themes of living water, light, and life, central to the ceremony of sacramental initiation to take place during the Easter Vigil, are to be the focus of prayer, reflection, and teaching during the period of purification and enlightenment.

Sacraments of Initiation

This is the high point of the initiation process, not its end. On Holy Saturday night, during the celebration of the Easter Vigil, the elected catechumens receive the sacraments of baptism, confirmation, and Eucharist during one and the same liturgical celebration.

This practice is in accord with the full rite of adult initiation. Again, this is understood as the model for all other practices of initiation.

THEOLOGICAL INTERLUDE

The close connection of baptism, confirmation, and Eucharist during one liturgical celebration has important theological significance.[5] This connection points to the unity of the paschal mystery, particularly the close relationship between the mission of the Son, Jesus Christ, and the outpouring of the Holy Spirit. Baptism is associated with the themes of death, rising, and incorporation into Christ. Confirmation is associated with enlightenment, empowerment, and strengthening by and in the Spirit. The joint celebration of the sacraments by which the Son and the Spirit come with the Father upon those who are initiated illustrates the unity of this mystery. In brief, one is not incorporated into Christ's dying and rising and into the new way of life which that sharing entails except through the power of the Spirit. The Holy Spirit's bestowal is precisely that which incorporates one into the mystery of Christ's Body. They are two sides of a coin. The close connection between the two, and their coming with the Father upon the initiated, is more effectively communicated when baptism and confirmation are celebrated in the same liturgical rite.

The theological significance is clearer when contrasted with older, yet still influential, theological positions which saw baptism rather exclusively in terms of *cleansing from sin* by incorporation into the passion, death, and Resurrection of Jesus. Confirmation was seen as *a strengthening to do battle against the forces of evil in the world*. Through confirmation one was thought to become a soldier for Christ. Baptism and confirmation were viewed not as distinct sacramental moments in one initiation process, but as two separate sacraments, each with its own cause and effect. Baptism did one thing, confirmation did something else. The *RCIA* stresses the intrinsic and inseparable unity of the mission of the Son and the Spirit by calling for a joint celebration of the sacraments.

Baptism and confirmation are closely connected with the Eucharist. Incorporation into the Body of Christ through the water of baptism and enlightenment by the Spirit through confirmation provide the basis for admission to the table of the Lord. In the same liturgical celebration in which they have been baptized and confirmed, the initiates are welcomed to the table of the Lord. Here again, the unity of the paschal mystery celebrated in the Eucharist is more clearly illustrated when all three sacraments are received in a joint celebration. The Eucharist is itself a sacrament of initiation. Our regular celebration of it week after week need not dull the awareness of our continuing need to be initiated ever more deeply into the mysteries of Christ's love and presence. In fact this repetition emphasizes initiation as process and the entire Christian community's need for ongoing conversion.

Postbaptismal Catechesis or Mystagogia

The need for ongoing conversion and initiation into Christ's mysteries is well illustrated in the stage of postbaptismal catechesis or mystagogia. Mystagogia refers to the teaching of the mysteries. This is a period of deepening and further intensification, the keynote of which is *ongoing conversion* in Christ and his mysteries. The rationale of this stage is that people understand and penetrate more deeply the meaning of something they have experienced. Prior to their sacramental initiation, the newly initiated had only *heard* about baptism and confirmation. They may have observed such celebrations previously, but they were celebrations of someone else's baptism or confirmation. The same is true of the Eucharist. Now initiated into the community, having received the sacraments of baptism, confirmation, and Eucharist, they are better able to understand the Christian mysteries about which they had previously only heard. This period of mystagogia ends at the close of Easter season marked by a celebration on Pentecost.

An example may serve to clarify the difference between the rationale of the earlier stages of catechesis and that of postbaptismal catechesis. Increasing numbers of couples who are expecting their first child are attending sessions in preparation for the birth. The physician explains to the couples what will occur during delivery, and the various strategies of self- and mutual help which will facilitate the process of birth. The participants ask questions; often these are of a theoretical sort, especially those posed by the fathers-to-be. Several weeks or months pass. The baby is born. In the follow-up session the physician's presentation is quite different from what it had been in previous sessions because the mind-set has changed: what these people had previously only heard spoken of, they now have experienced quite concretely. On the part of the participants there are few, if any, questions of a theoretical nature.

Mystagogia points to the experiential nature of sacramental initiation as well as to the process of initiation as ongoing, a process which does not end with the waters of baptism, the anointing in the

Spirit in confirmation, or the bread and wine of the Eucharist. Like conversion, initiation into the Christian mysteries ends at death.

Analysis of the RCIA

Examination of the *RCIA* raises several points of interest, particularly if one is more familiar with other forms of Christian initiation, such as the baptism of infants. Again, although the rite was released over fifteen years ago and proposed as a model for all forms of Christian initiation, it has not taken root in the liturgical life of the Roman Catholic community to the extent that many have suggested it should.[6] Before moving on to the question of the practice of baptizing infants, which becomes something of a problem when using the *RCIA* as a model for all Christian initiation, three points should be attended to.

Proper Unity and Sequence

The most striking point about the sacraments of initiation as they are found in the rite is the unity and sequence in which they are to be celebrated. There is increasing agreement among a good number of sacramental and liturgical theologians that baptism, confirmation, and Eucharist as sacraments of initiation should be celebrated together, most appropriately during the liturgy of Holy Saturday night.[7] This unity is crucial because of the connection between the mission of the Son and the mission of the Spirit. Many would agree that this unity is to be maintained in sacramental initiation whatever the age of the person being initiated. It is rooted in the earliest practice of the church. It has been maintained in the churches of the East. Roman Catholics are often quite startled while participating in liturgies of the Byzantine rite, to find, for example, that whole families with children of all ages, including infants in arms, present themselves to receive the Eucharist. In such churches infants are initiated by receiving the sacraments of baptism, confirmation, and Eucharist, in that sequence, during one liturgical celebration.

What is important here is to note that early Christian churches of both East and West practiced initiation through water bath, chrismation, and admission to the table. The early churches did not envision three separate sacraments of baptism, confirmation, and Eucharist. Rather, the water bath, sealing with chrism and hand laying, and participation in the Lord's Supper were more properly understood as three sacramental moments in a unified scheme of initiation. It would have been inconceivable for the early Christian churches to baptize and confirm someone without admitting her or him to the table of the Eucharist.

OBJECTIONS TO ORDER AND SEQUENCE

Often the argument is put forth that Eucharist should be withheld because infants and young children cannot understand its meaning. The same argument is sometimes used in defense of withholding the Eucharist from mentally handicapped persons. To this argument it must be said simply but quite firmly: if the argument that age or lack of understanding provides a basis for exclusion from the Eucharist, then the same argument must apply to baptism. Does the same infant, child, or mentally retarded person have a sense or knowledge of baptism and its meaning when baptized? Is sufficient knowledge of the meaning of baptism not required if one requires such sufficient knowledge for the reception of the Eucharist? Fundamentally, this whole concern with age and sufficient knowledge places far too much stress upon one's *worthiness* to receive and celebrate sacraments, and overlooks the nature of all sacramental life, and the Eucharist in particular, as gift which is freely offered precisely in light of our unworthiness.

Again, the unity and sequence proposed by the rite finds root in the earliest practices of the churches. The corporate unity of the ritual of initiation disintegrated and became disjoined as the years of the early church passed. This was the result of various historical factors which cannot be treated here.[8] It is enough to say that the disintegration and dismemberment of the rite of initiation were more a historical accident than a goal to which the churches moved reflectively and with a sense of clear purpose. What was once a single ritual of initiation through baptism, confirmation, and Eucharist came to be viewed as three separate sacraments, each with its own cause and effect.

Further, not only was the integral unity of the rite dismembered: the natural sequence of the rite was broken by placing first penance before first Eucharist. Confirmation came to be celebrated well after first Eucharist. This was largely due to continued insistence in the Christian West that the *bishop* should confirm. In the early days of the church, the bishop presided over sacramental initiation and, consequently, was the one to confirm. But with the increase in numbers of Christians, and therefore an increase in initiation ceremonies, the bishop could not be present at each initiation ceremony. The Western Christian churches chose to reserve confirmation for the bishop, who would confirm on his next visit to a particular community. Because of the growth of Christianity, which resulted in the geographical expansion of dioceses, the bishop's visit was delayed often quite considerably—often months and years. The result was the emergence of the separate sacrament of confirmation, which seemed more a dangling sacramental participle than the sealing of the Spirit given in baptism.

What was considered normal, "traditional" sacramental practice prior to the Second Vatican Council is not traditional in the richest sense of the term. The practice of baptism, followed by penance in preparation for Eucharist, followed by confirmation sometimes years later, is far removed from the early practice of initiation in the church. It is to this earlier tradition, with its sound theological base and deep symbolic sensitivity, that the contemporary church urges us to return through the promulgation of the *RCIA* as model of initiation.

Church as Community

Based on the examination of the *RCIA*, it is clear that a requirement for initiation is a living and vibrant community into which one is initiated. In speaking of community the rite envisions a *group of people who are willing to share their lives.* A community is a group which, though it may vary in number, comes together in self- and mutual help. A Christian community is one in which prayer is shared together with the joys and sorrows of life. Such sharing occurs primarily through the exploration and continual rediscovery of the gospel message of Jesus Christ and by participation in his mysteries. Through their sharing of discipline, celebration, sorrow, and mission, the community becomes a corporate witness and sign to and in the world.[9]

It is to be regretted that many Catholic groupings do not envision themselves in such a way; even more that many, including those in leadership in the church, would look to such an experience of church as repulsive, at odds with the religion which they have grown up in, and which they cherish so dearly. Consequently, as it stands now, it is usually the case that people can be partially *assimilated into* the church, but they cannot be truly *initiated.* This is so because local churches seem to function more like aggregates or loose affiliations, rather than communities as envisioned in the *RCIA.* One's understanding of initiation depends in large measure upon one's understanding of the church. If the church is seen primarily as hierarchy and assistants who dispense sacraments, then initiation thus described will be seen as superfluous. From this point of view what is foremost is the reception of the sacraments, in any way, shape, or form, so that the desired grace might be granted. If church and liturgy are seen primarily as obligation, then the lengthy participation in the initiatory process will be looked upon as a burden on both time and efficiency. If, however, the church is viewed as Body of Christ which expresses and receives its life and mission in the sacramental celebrations of the church, then the process of initiation, and the conversion which it requires, will be viewed as part of the church's ongoing conversion in Christ and an opportunity for deeper initiation into his love and presence. One's vision of initiation depends upon one's vision of church.

An Experiential Process

As envisioned by the *RCIA*, initiation is a process which is primarily experiential and secondarily instructional. In a former day, the approach to sacramental preparation and catechesis was highly cognitive with a strong emphasis upon memorization and accountability to the priest or pastor. The focus in a contemporary approach to sacramental preparation and catechesis based on the *RCIA* is not primarily on theories, objective truths, or facts to be memorized. Knowledge of the mysteries at the core of the community's faith, its teachings, as well as active participation in the community's service of others, is essential. Catechesis, as both instruction and learning, is understood as an experience which is lifelong and which implies the daily task of conversion in Christ and the continuing effort, shared with others, to live out of the church's understanding of itself as the People of God through grace and by the power of the Spirit.

The Question of Infant Baptism

The baptism of infants is a practice with a long history. In the beginning baptism required choice and conversion; consequently, baptism was restricted to adults. As time went on infants and children were first baptized as members of households of faith. They were not baptized alone, in isolation from the family. The patristic period is marked by extraordinary theological sophistication, shaped by a strong preoccupation with sin. This can be seen in the figure of Augustine. In him we find a full-blown treatment of original sin and an urgent and impassioned plea for the baptism of infants. The practice of baptizing infants developed slowly, gradually, and sporadically, but it did finally take hold. It gained and maintained priority over adult baptism in most of the history of Western Christianity.[10]

If the *RCIA* is accepted as the model of Christian initiation, then important questions are raised regarding the current practice of the baptism of infants and children. The questions emerge primarily because the whole focus of the *RCIA* as a model is an adult focus, and its whole principle and rationale is conversion in Christ. In what sense can we speak of the conversion of infants?

The practice of infant baptism has continued since the promulgation of the *RCIA*. It is a practice which has become very deeply rooted in the Christian psyche and in Christian practice. Given that infant baptism is a continuing practice, what can we learn about this practice vis-à-vis what the *RCIA* as a model says about the nature of all Christian initiation?

First, the proper order and sequence of the sacraments of initiation must be maintained. If infants are baptized, then the next sacrament to be received, at whatever age it is received, is confirmation. Confirmation is to be followed by Eucharist. This would allow for the practice of infant baptism while respecting the order and sequence, if not the inherent unity, of sacramental initiation which is found in the *RCIA*.

Second, because the dynamic of conversion forms the heart and soul of Christian initiation, attention must be given to the fact that, although one may be baptized in infancy, initiation is a process which takes place over a considerable period of time. This occurs within the context of a supportive, nurturing community of faith. The process is set in motion when the infant is baptized. It does not end until death. The responsibilities of Christian life and conversion are not held in abeyance until the child goes off to Catholic school or religious instruction class. This same point is also made in the *Rite of Baptism for Children*,[11] addressing the issue of the preparation of parents, sponsors, and community for the baptism of infants.

A third possibility resides in the implementation of the Scottsdale statement (1973) on Christian initiation for children of responsible parents. Two different patterns could coexist: the full rite of initiation of infants followed by catechesis appropriate to subsequent stages of development; or enrollment of infants as catechumens, with initiation to be celebrated at a later age after catechesis. Instead of postponing confirmation until adolescence, other rituals appropriate to celebrating Christian decision and commitment might be implemented.[12]

Ethical Implications of the
Sacraments of Initiation

The ethical implications of the sacraments emerge in light of the morality which the sacraments themselves express. The purpose in speaking of ethical implications is not to point to specific things that one has to do or must do. The approach here is not prescriptive: no prescribed formulas for behavior emerge from giving attention to the morality expressed in sacrament. But the particular ethical implications which derive from the view of Christian morality expressed in the sacraments of initiation may be spelled out briefly in terms of covenant, fidelity, responsibility, care for the weak and wounded, and justice for all.

In baptism one is initiated into a *covenant morality* through incorporation into Christ's death and Resurrection. Such sharing calls for a new way of life based on the covenant. This is a morality or ethic which is rooted in *love and fidelity*, not *law or obligation*. The ethic is shaped by a sense of responsibility to God and others, not obligation or requirement. This is a responsibility which arises as a result of membership in God's people through baptism. It is a morality grounded in relationship to others in community, and to Christ the Lord. Moral life entails the ongoing task of viewing one's life and actions, and those of others, in light of the Lordship of Jesus Christ so that the ongoing conversion in Christ begun in baptism may be brought to completion. Everything and everyone is to be seen in light of this Lordship. Because the life and ministry of Jesus was focused upon the poor and wounded, the sick and the outcast, the nameless and the abhorred, those who are incorporated into his Body in baptism are to give pride of place to the poor and the weak, the wounded and the forgotten, the oppressed and the violated. Such persons and their needs become primary in the lives of those who struggle to live by the grace and Spirit given in baptism. The little and the weak, the forgotten and the powerless are, in line with the promise of Jesus, first in the reign of God. Christian moral life entails working to create a world, both now and to come, in which all may grow, with special predilection for the least of our sisters and brothers.

The sealing of the Spirit in confirmation is the sacramental act by which a person and the whole community recognize and submit to the attraction and leading of the Spirit. Confirmation is not primarily the sacrament of choice or commitment as is often thought. It signals abandonment and submission to the power of the Spirit. One abandoned to the sway and power of the Spirit is led to live according to the Spirit, not according to the flesh. By their fruits, you will know them. Their lives are marked by peace, patience, kindness, long-suffering, gentleness, faithfulness, single-hearted love of God and neighbor. The absence of the Spirit is recognized in hatred, jealousy, envy, greed, lust, and despair.

Notes

1. Promulgated as *Ordo Initiationis Christianae Adultorum* by the Sacred Congregation for Divine Worship (6 January 1972). Referred to hereafter as *RCIA*.

2. See *Made, Not Born: New Perspectives on Christian Initiation and the Catechumenate*, The Murphy Center for Liturgical Research (Notre Dame, IN: University of Notre Dame Press, 1976). Several of the articles in this collection of essays make this claim.

3. Readers whose religious education took place prior to or during the Second Vatican Council will be readily familiar with this catechism. The Baltimore Catechism was the standard tool for catechesis prior to Vatican II, and relied very heavily on the memorization of specific answers to particular religious questions.

4. Aidan Kavanagh, *The Shape of Baptism: The Rite of Christian Initiation*, (New York: Pueblo Publishing Co., 1978), p. 102ff; see also pp. 126–27. Kevin Irwin, among others, does not accept the normativity of the *RCIA* for Christian initiatory practice. See Irwin's "Christian Initiation: Some Important Questions," *The Chicago Catechumenate* 3, no. 3 (March 1981): 4–24.

5. For insights on the theological significance of the joint celebration of baptism, confirmation, and Eucharist, I am indebted to the work of Aidan Kavanagh, *The Shape of Baptism*, p. 134ff.; see espec. p. 138.

6. See Ralph Keifer, "Christian Initiation: The State of the Question," in *Made, Not Born*, pp. 138–51.

7. Kavanagh, *The Shape of Baptism*, p. 134ff.

8. For a fuller treatment of this point see Nathan Mitchell, "Dissolution of the Rite of Christian Initiation," in *Made, Not Born*, pp. 50–82.

9. Robert Hovda, "Hope for the Future: A Summary," in *Made, Not Born*, pp. 152–67; see espec. pp. 159–60.

10. See *Instruction on Infant Baptism* (20 October 1980). Herein the Congregation for the Doctrine of the Faith clearly affirms the importance of infant baptism.

11. Originally promulgated by the Sacred Congregation for Divine Worship as *Ordo Baptismi Parvulorum* (15 May 1969).

12. Gerard Austin, *Anointing with the Spirit: The Rite of Confirmation* (New York: Pueblo Publishing Co., 1985), p. 126ff. For more about the Scottsdale statement, see John Gallen, "American Liturgy: A Theological Locus," *Theological Studies* 35, no. 2 (1974): 302–11; see espec. pp. 307–8.

5

Eucharist

The liturgy is viewed by the Second Vatican Council as the fountain and summit of the life of the Catholic community. This is particularly true of the Eucharist. It is the sacramental act to which the other sacraments lead and from which they flow. Baptism and confirmation are steps in the initiation process which comes to fulfillment at the table of the Lord. Penance is the sacrament whereby Christians are reconciled with the community which worships God and receives its identity as Body of Christ in the Eucharist. Both anointing and penance are sacraments of healing and reconciliation. But these can only be properly understood when seen in light of the Eucharist as the fundamental sacramental expression of God's healing and reconciling love. The Body of Christ which is proclaimed and celebrated uniquely in the Eucharist is built and served through ministry, ordained and nonordained, and through the community of love in marriage. The sacraments of initiation incorporate the believer into a eucharistic community which is built and served through the many ministries, ordained and nonordained, and by the love and fidelity of husband and wife in marriage. The healing and sanctifying grace which is celebrated in the Eucharist finds particular expression in the sacraments of anointing and penance.

Eucharist: Ongoing Initiation in Christ

From our previous study of the *RCIA*, we are aware of the importance of conversion in the process of initiation. It should also be clear that the conversion process does not end with the reception of the sacraments of baptism, confirmation, and Eucharist. The role of the postbaptismal catechesis after the reception of the sacraments makes clear the need for ongoing conversion in Christian life. This need finds its focus in the Eucharist by which the Christian community continually discovers itself as the People of God, the Body of Christ. The Eucharist is the sacramental act by which the Christian community is initiated over and over again into the mysteries of Christ's presence and love. Christian initiation ends only at death. Yet even at the point of death the Eucharist is again seen as source and summit, for it is the Eucharist—viaticum, food for the journey—which is given at the moment of initiation to a new mode of existence beyond death.[1]

Eucharist, together with baptism, has enjoyed priority in the sacramental life of the church. Some theologians in the church's history have tried to stress the difference between the Eucharist and the other sacraments with unfortunate consequences, for the Eucharist is not the only sacrament which effectively communicates Christ's presence. It belongs alongside the other sacraments, as well as alongside Scripture and other manifestations of God's presence, such as ikons. The Eucharist is more deeply symbolic than other sacraments in that all other sacraments derive their meaning from their relationship to it, and have their purpose in drawing Christians more fully into its celebration. The Eucharist differs from other sacraments because it is the gathering and celebration of the Body of Christ, the center where the church comes to full expression. In the Eucharist the Christian community finds the focal point which brings together in common expression of faith and celebration all of the symbols that belong to the mystery of Christ in the church.

In this sense Christian living may be said to be not only sacramental but also an expression of a eucharistic spirituality. Authentic Christian life emerges when communities of faith who receive and express their identity in the breaking of bread and sharing of cup attempt to live by the Lordship of Jesus Christ and the empowerment of the Spirit celebrated in the Eucharist.

The Eucharist and the Tradition of the Meal

Prior to explanations and definitions, and before trying to master the highly refined and nuanced nomenclature of eucharistic theology, if the Eucharist is to be understood, it must be appreciated for what it is at the most basic level: the Eucharist is a ritual meal. At the level of human significance the meal serves to nourish and sustain life. It binds and unites persons to the earth, to all of creation, to family, friends, community, to the race, and to the cosmos. The meal is central to the life of a family or group because it provides occasion for coming together and for nourishing. Not only are bodies nourished, but identities of families or groups are nourished and strengthened as well. Friends share meals. Strangers ordinarily do not. Persons unknown to one another eat in the same restaurant, but they do not share a meal. Eating a meal with others lends to interpersonal communion and communication. But this interpersonal sharing occurs precisely because of the very concrete and basic need for the material substance which provides the occasion for coming together: food and drink.

The Meal in Jewish Tradition

If the Eucharist is to be understood, it is not enough to look at the human significance of the meal, though that is where we begin. It is the meal tradition in Judaism, a religious tradition, which provides the context for a proper understanding of the Christian Eucharist.

The meanings which are associated with the meal at the basic human level are also found in the Jewish understanding of the Passover meal which celebrates the Exodus and covenant. Life, sustenance, bonding, family, friendship are all given and strengthened in the very simple and fundamental activity of taking a meal together. But all of these elements take on a new significance when the meal provides the occasion for the historical commemoration of the Exodus and covenant. These fundamental meanings associated with meal are not set aside but are seen from the perspective of belief in the God who is active in history and present to creation. This God has taken the side of this people, has chosen them from among all people, has established a bond with them and among themselves, has promised them long life and many children, and given them a land of their own. The eating of the meal, which at the most basic level signifies life, bonding, family, and friendship is taken up and charged with religious significance. This significance is shaped by the belief in God's activity on their behalf in the Exodus and covenant. The meal itself then becomes a sharing, a bonding, a transmission of life, and a strengthening of the faith of the Jewish community.

The meal in the Jewish community of faith provides the occasion for historical remembrance. The Exodus and covenant which brought about the freedom and corporate liberation of the Jews are remembered precisely through participation in the meal of the covenant—the sharing of the story of the Jewish people together with the sharing of food and drink.

The seeds of a particularly Christian community of faith lie in the Resurrection of the crucified one. Like the Exodus / covenant, the raising of the crucified was for the early followers of Jesus an experience of liberation and freedom. It was an experience of a continuing offer of emancipation and of hope. This faith differed from Jewish faith because, aside from discerning God's activity in history and God's presence to creation, the new faith looked to such activity and presence in a person. Despite the difference, however, the meal, with all its basic human significance and its central role in the religious life of Judaism, became central when the followers of Jesus expressed their faith in the God of Jesus Christ.

It is clearer now due to recent developments in biblical exegesis that what we recognize as the Christian Eucharist developed out of a Judaism which, at the time of Jesus, had many different types of religious meals. It is not at all certain that the Christian Eucharist is continuous in the line of the Passover, or covenant meal. What is brought into the Christian tradition from Judaism is the centrality of the meal itself, the quintessential importance of sharing food and drink as focus for historical commemoration. But the Christian Eucharist is not simply the covenant meal with a Christian difference.

Food and Drink in the New Testament

It is now more commonly recognized that there are no easy answers to the question of the origins of the Eucharist. We have already seen (chap. 2) some of the problems which arise when there is an easy and unchecked reliance upon a narrow view of the institution of the sacraments.

Of all the sacraments, those which are readily supported by New Testament evidence are baptism and Eucharist. What are commonly referred to as the "institution narratives," those passages from Scripture which tell of the Last Supper and which are now part of the eucharistic prayer of the Mass, are usually singled out as focuses for our understanding of the Eucharist. Yet even the narratives of the Last Supper need to be seen in a new light, and within a much broader horizon. In themselves they neither express the full significance of the Eucharist nor give adequate account of its origins. The so-called institution narratives must be read in light of other meal stories in the New Testament which involve Jesus. All of these together may be looked at as disclosive of his meaning and message and, consequently, of the significance of the Eucharist. While the stories of the Last Supper may have a special importance and express the significance of the Eucharist in unique and particular ways, this significance can be enriched, rather than diminished, when seen alongside a whole array of other meal stories, which tell of Jesus.

Jesus eats with sinners (Luke 5:29–32; Mark 2:15–17; Matt. 9:10–13), thereby indicating his willingness to be in a relationship of communion with them. The sharing of a meal with them indicates sharing of life and the strengthening of a bond with outcasts: those at the margins of society and religious institutions. The multiplication of loaves (Matt. 15:32–39; Mark 6:30–44; 8:1–10) points out Jesus' attention to basic human needs and to the necessity of caring for those who are hungry. In the story of the raising of the daughter of Jairus (Mark 5:21–43) he is again depicted as one concerned for the needs of the little and the weak. The spiritual strength which has been given to the daughter in raising her up is insufficient. Those present are asked to give her something to eat to nourish her body. The meal table is itself crucial to the way in which Jesus is depicted (Luke 14:7–24) and becomes a means of communicating his message. Disciples are to take the lowest place at the table. When a party is given, the poor, the crippled, the lame, the blind are to be invited, those who cannot return the favor. Everyone, even those ordinarily unwelcome, has a place at the table. In the Emmaus story (Luke 24:13–35) Jesus is recognized by the disciples in the taking, blessing, and giving of bread.

The meal stories are not to be understood as lesser types or vague figures of the stories of the Last Supper. More than likely, an early understanding of the Eucharist is presented in the meal stories and in the way Jesus is depicted with food and drink as much as in the story of the Last Supper.

Food and Drink of the Christian Meal

Though deeply rooted in the Jewish practice of the commemorative meal, the Christian Eucharist differs from Jewish practice in that aside from remembering a person, Jesus, it is a much simpler meal. From early on the food and drink of the Christian meal have been bread and wine. Sharing bread and wine means sharing life and destiny at a very fundamental level. The simplicity of elements also discloses the message and meaning of Jesus. No one needs to feel out of place at the table. All can come, all can be present, and no one needs to be mindful of etiquette, in a manner of speaking, because this is sharing of the most elementary sort. There is room for all at the table, as the life and testament of Jesus bear witness. There was a place even for Judas at the table the night before Jesus died.

Precisely because they are simple and basic, the elements of bread and wine are appropriate for use in the Christian meal. In the context of the Christian meal, however, bread and wine are used symbolically. In accord with the nature of symbol, the elements which common sense recognizes as bread and wine take on many meanings. Wine strengthens, but it can also weaken and destroy. It builds bonds, but can also break them. It makes for light hearts and tears. There is the wine of delight, the wine of the Jewish Pasch, the cup of salvation to be taken up while calling on the name of the Lord. There is the wine of Cana, the cup of the Last Supper, and the cup from which life eternal springs.

Bread nourishes. With it people are gathered at table and fed. Bread can be given or withheld. It delights human hearts. Yet there is the bread of tears. There is the bread of manna in the desert, the bread of the Pasch, the bread which was multiplied, the loaf broken with the disciples. And there is the bread promised for the life of the world.

When used in the Eucharist, bread and wine disclose all these meanings, and more. Though one or another meaning may be highlighted, each is enriched when seen in light of the many meanings which bread and wine have borne in Jewish and Christian uses. Liturgy suffers when there is an effort to pin down the significance of bread or of wine to just one meaning. Attempts to limit the significance of liturgical symbols to one, preconceived meaning violate the efficacy of these symbolic realities. A focal meaning may be helpful, but this meaning can be complemented and enriched by other meanings which are deeply rooted in the human and Christian stories. For example, the focal image of sacrifice as it pertains to Eucharist, which has much to recommend it when understood in light of the historical and cultural context within which it gained prominence,[2] must be viewed in light of the other meanings of bread and wine as these have been treated above. It is an impoverishment when a community neglects to remember the bread of affliction, the bread of manna in the desert, and the bread which David took from the tabernacle. All of these images belong within the context of eucharistic celebration. Such images must be retrieved in the way that Christian communities remember. The history of liturgy reminds us that even when a single meaning seems to capture and express the complete significance of the liturgical symbols, a return to the multiplicity of meanings can give rise to a fresh and a richer understanding of the meaning of the Eucharist.

Memory: The Heart of Eucharist

Fundamentally Eucharist is an invitation to share at the table of the Lord. It is a memorial, an act of remembering. Eucharist is a partaking of the Body and the Blood of the Lord in the breaking of bread and the sharing of a cup. The remembering which forms the heart and soul of the Eucharist is an act; it is dynamic. Different communities remember Jesus differently, thus giving rise to varying understandings of Christ, church, and ministry. This act of remembrance takes place at the table of remembrance and in the hearing of the word which recounts God's activity and presence to creation. Remembering gives rise to thanksgiving for the gift given in Jesus and his Spirit. The great prayer of thanksgiving, the eucharistic prayer, expresses our remembering as we are ourselves transformed into Christ's Body through this remembrance and through the empowerment of the Holy Spirit.

Memory is the heart of the Eucharist. Since this is so, attention must be given to different ways of remembering Jesus in eucharistic celebration. A glance at the various churches of the apostolic age reveals that there was not one uniform, universal understanding of Christ from the beginning. Rather, a variety of perceptions of his meaning and message were spawned early on in the churches because of the different ways Christ was remembered. Since he was remembered differently by various communities, the church and its ministry were understood differently according to the way in which Christ was remembered. For example, remembering Jesus as the forsaken, suffering servant results in a type of church life and exercise of ministry different from that which emerges as a result of remembering Christ primarily in terms of his kingship or sovereignty over all history and peoples.

In our own day the churches are called to active remembrance of Christ in ways that take account of the needs and urgent demands of our age, and in light of what is revealed in the various depictions of Jesus in the Gospels. Christian communities must be suspicious of some currents within the tradition which have tended to forget certain challenging and discomforting elements of the Jesus story.[3] Hence there must be a conscious choice to remember what we would sometimes rather forget. There needs to be a choice not to forget: for example, what the various stories of food and drink say about the demanding nature of Christian life and about the requirements for participation in the community's worship. Those tendencies to remember Jesus' sacrifice for sin, but to forget his relationship to sinners, must be criticized; as well, those currents in traditional and contemporary practice which selectively remember the Twelve at the Last Supper, but deliberately forget the many meals which Jesus shared with women, thus inviting them to a share in his life and ministry. We must ask if, in our remembering the Jesus who called the Twelve and set them aside for a particular ministry, we have forgotten that the message of Jesus is one which allows no room for distinction of persons based on rank or status.

Perhaps no way of remembering Jesus is more suited to present need and contemporary perceptions of God, humanity, and the world than is the understanding of Jesus as God's own compassion.[4] In the person of Jesus, God enters into complete solidarity with the victims of oppression, with the wounded, those trampled underfoot, the little, the weak, and the forgotten. Jesus empties himself (Phil. 2:6–11) and enters into solidarity with victims unto death and into hell. To remember Jesus in this way entails calling to memory the victims of all ages who have been forgotten. It also implies our willingness to stand in solidarity with them, recognizing that they hold pride of place in the reign of God.[5]

The understanding of the church which emerges from this way of remembering is one which gives prominence to the little, the weak, and the suffering. It is these who reveal God's compassion in Jesus in a unique and particular manner. The hallmarks of such an understanding of church are People of God, service, charism, and prophecy.[6] Ministry is understood not primarily in terms of power, authority, and jurisdiction, but in terms of service, self-emptying, compassion, and care. Such an understanding of Christ, church, and ministry, well supported by the New Testament and by precedents in the history of the church, is the one which contemporary churches must struggle to remember most of all.

Shape of the Eucharist:
From Table of Remembrance to Sacrifice of the Mass

As we have seen, the bread and wine of the Jewish meal tradition were carried over into the Christian meal in which the crucified and risen one was remembered. His life was continually conveyed in this way, and his meaning and message communicated in the sharing of simple and basic food and drink. Originally the Eucharist was understood as a commemorative meal, much like the Jewish Passover, and was unencumbered by other layers of meaning which later came to dominate eucharistic life and theology.

In the third chapter we saw that the establishment of the new faith as a state-approved religion in the early part of the fourth century brought with it a departure from some of the early practices of Christian worship, which were noticeably biased against the ritual of the temple, cult, and priesthood. The earliest Christians had no priesthood and no sacrifice other than the remembrance of Jesus in the breaking of bread and the passing of the cup, their obedience to the gospel, and their praise of God.

But with the cultural adaptation of Christian faith these central realities were often obscured, and the spiritual freedom which characterized early worship was increasingly restricted in a process of resacralization. In the effort to adapt itself to a variety of cultural models Christian faith and practice were influenced by the practices of pagan temple worship and by some currents in Jewish worship. Hence elements such as priesthood and cult, central to these other forms of worship, influenced Christian life and liturgical practice.

It is through this process of resacralization that the language of sacrifice came to be used in reference to the Eucharist. Remembrance of Christ took a turn which emphasized the sacrificial reparation for human sin which Jesus offered by his death. This kind of remembrance resulted in a form of worship which looked at the Eucharist primarily in terms of sacrifice and priesthood. Its influence is still felt today.

The image of sacrifice has been central to the Christian understanding of Eucharist since the patristic period. Although the patristic period, with its deep symbolic sensitivity, maintained the metaphorical understanding of sacrifice, this was not always kept to the fore in later Western patterns of eucharistic life and theology.[7] Vulgarization of the image of sacrifice prevailed in the Middle Ages: popular naive realism looked at the Eucharist as sacrifice in a quite literal sense, which had very negative effects in the life of the church. This vulgarization with its preoccupation with the physical and material dimension of eucharistic sacrifice went hand in hand with enormous numbers of the faithful absenting themselves from eucharistic communion. The sacrifice which necessitated priest and cult, but little else, took the place of the realities of gathering, assembling, and participating.

Such negative effects of a literal, or naive, interpretation should not blind us to the positive elements which the image of Eucharist as sacrifice brought to the life of the church. In highlighting Eucharist as sacrifice, the people came to see themselves united with the death of Christ. Eucharist as sacrifice provided the possibility for identifying with and participating in the suffering and passion of Christ, which brought with it a sense of hope and confidence in the *promise of his Resurrection*. United to the death of Christ in such a way, believers understood themselves to be giving glory to God, and offered themselves as a living sacrifice of praise to God. Further, the image of sacrifice helped to bring about social cohesion in the church. Whatever one may care to say about the negative effect of the liturgy prior

to Vatican II, it pulled believers together, and kept them together—
due in large part to the central image of sacrifice which united
believers everywhere, past, present, and to come.

But to recognize and admire the accomplishments of the past is
not necessarily the same as advocating a return to past practices.
Because the imagery of sacrifice had positive effects in the history of
the development of the Eucharist does not guarantee that Eucharist
as sacrifice needs to have a central place in contemporary thought and
practice. It is simply important to note, especially in an age grown
impatient with the customs of other persons, communities, and
epochs, that what is often looked upon as outdated or old-fashioned
served a useful purpose and provided meaning for other persons in
other ages. New is not always better; old is not always worse. Perhaps
we can only understand the strengths and weaknesses of a contemporary approach to Eucharist, or to any subject for that matter, if we
are willing to look at other practices and persons on their own terms,
in light of their own historical situation. Judgment about Christian
practice is to be made on the basis of whether such practice provides
a sense of meaning and purpose in light of the Lordship of Jesus
Christ. To speak of a contemporary approach to Eucharist, or to the
other sacraments, is not to discard the contributions of former
epochs, but to learn from these insights and bring them into a
comprehensive and contemporary understanding of how God relates
to human beings, and how they relate to God.

A Contemporary Approach to Eucharist

Contemporary approaches to the Eucharist look upon the practices of the early churches as models of eucharistic practice. There is
a deeper understanding, therefore, of the Eucharist as a ritual of
broken bread and shared cup. The focal point is commemorative
meal. The aim is to retrieve the earlier elements of assembling as a
community of faith, sharing and praying in thanksgiving. Commemoration and narrative play a vital role as illustrated in the significance
given to the proclamation and hearing of the word, and the narrative
character of the great prayer of thanksgiving, the eucharistic prayer.

Whereas in the past few centuries Catholics felt united with
Christ in offering his sacrifice irrespective of whether they took
communion, today we have a sense of being in communion with his
sacrifice through sacramental communion, of being transformed
through communion in his death and Resurrection in the eating and
drinking of his Body and Blood. This is to join together the notions of

sacrifice and meal, as sacrificial meal, as well as to accentuate the prayer of memorial thanksgiving as the most perfect sacrifice that Christians can make.

With the recovery of these elements it is now more commonly recognized that naive generalizations about the differences between Roman Catholics and other Christians on the nature of the Eucharist cannot be accepted. The World Council of Churches' Faith and Order Commission[8] presents an understanding of the Eucharist which we will follow in articulating a contemporary Roman Catholic approach to the Eucharist. Be it noted, however, that the Roman Catholic church has no official representation in the World Council of Churches. This in no way lessens the significance of this understanding of Eucharist and what it might lend to a Roman Catholic understanding.

Memorial

Above all else, Eucharist is a memorial in the sense that it is the activity of remembering, *anamnesis*.[9] This derives from the account of the Lord's Supper which includes the invitation to "do this as a memorial of me" (e.g., Luke 22:19). But this description can be applied to all prayers and rituals insofar as all prayers and rituals are part of remembrance. To remember is not simply to recall. The key to understanding Christian liturgy is that acts of worship are done in memory of past salvific events, so that those gathered in remembrance may participate in them and receive the promises they offer in the present. This understanding of memorial is central in the narratives of the Last Supper in the Gospels and in the writings of Paul. In the Gospels of Luke and John there is also the dimension of personal memory. Jesus asks that he be remembered as one who is among them as a servant. This is the witness he leaves to those who follow him.

Christian memory is focused not only on God who acts in history for the salvation of all. It is directed to a person, Jesus Christ, in whom God is active and present. The narration of God's action in history and presence to creation finds its place alongside remembrance of the one whose life was given to the service of those whom he called brothers and sisters: the little, weak, wounded, outcast, sinners, the forgotten, and the nameless. To remember Jesus is thus to remember them and to respond to the call and challenge offered in and through them.

Thanksgiving

The prayer of thanksgiving, or the eucharistic prayer, expresses the remembrance which is at the heart of liturgy. In it a new vision of reality is proclaimed from the perspective of God's love and good-ness. The past is recalled, and all events of history are told in light of the awareness of grace and sin in human life and history. God is blessed and thanked for bringing the people to the present day. Protection is asked. God's blessing is called upon those present, while grace and Spirit are invoked so as to enable those gathered to wait in hope and confidence, and to work for the coming of the reign of God. To re-member is to be thankful for what God has done in hope and confi-dence that God will be faithful to the promise given in Jesus Christ.

In our own day we are faced with the suffering of millions and with the death of thousands and thousands by senseless violence. We are confronted with the senselessness and meaninglessness of our age signaled in the twofold holocaust. In light of this, the remembrance of Jesus Christ which is at the heart of the Eucharist must give voice to sorrow and lamentation as well as to thanksgiving. In lamentation a community's experience of suffering, pain, and sorrow is expressed and in such self-expression they can be transformed.

Lamentation "names" or articulates the community's percep-tion of human sin and the forces of evil which prohibit the free reception of and response to God's grace and word. Pain and disillu-sionment are voiced, and expectations which have dimmed are brought to expression. This sense of lamentation was and remains vital to the Jewish people and to their liturgy. It must be retrieved and allowed to come to the center of Christian assemblies.

Lamentation is not endless complaining. It carries the seed of hope. It looks in hope to the poor and forgotten, and all who live at the edges of society and religious institutions in light of the promise of God's vindication.[10]

Lamentation leads to praise and thanksgiving; for it is possible to accept one's sin and sinfulness only where there is a trace of hope. Whatever is remembered in lamentation, in crying out before God's face, is renewed and redeemed. To lament is to look at God's promise and to voice the desire and urgent longing for God which is yet unfulfilled. Thus lamentation in the biblical sense is at the same time an act of thanksgiving for the promise given in Jesus Christ which is being brought to completion by grace and Spirit.

Invocation of the Spirit

The eucharistic celebration unites in one action the presence and activity of Christ in the church through the invocation of the Spirit, *epiclesis*.[11] The Spirit is that in us which enables us to call God

"Abba." Spirit describes the very life of God which dwells in each one of us. It is the Spirit of Jesus which lives on in the life of the church through initiation and participation in the life and practice of the Christian community, and which makes faith possible. The Spirit sanctifies, makes holy, both the assembly gathered at the table and the bread and wine which are placed upon it. This sanctification by the Spirit is well expressed in the words of the Mass: "Grant that we, who are nourished by his body and blood, may be filled with his Holy Spirit, and become one body, one spirit in Christ."[12] Through the invocation of the Spirit the Christian community is transformed into the Body of Christ by the unity of love and charity which the Spirit brings, and by the activity of service which life in the Spirit requires.

Communion of the Faithful

The Eucharist is not the activity of the ordained alone. It is a community's act of remembrance through grace and Spirit. In such remembrance through word and worship, a particular assembly is joined in the communion of faith throughout the world, and in union with people of all ages past, present, and to come. The Eucharist is the corporate action of faith done in response to God's invitation in Jesus Christ. This response is expressed in various modes of prayer, through which the Spirit illumines the minds and hearts of those assembled and enables them to do what is true in love. The gathering and celebration of the Body of Christ, the eucharistic liturgy is the action wherein the church takes its true form.

Meal of the Reign of God

The Eucharist is an anticipatory symbol of the reign of God. What is promised as yet to come is given to some degree in the communion of faith which is celebrated. The reign of God, central to the message of Jesus, is a way of expressing God's intention for the world both now and to come. It is a message of forgiveness, mercy, kindness, justice, and peace. This is the future promised by Christ. According to this promise, the "underprivileged" are the privileged; the poor and the downtrodden will be first in the reign of God.

As the anticipation of the coming reign of God wherein the poor and wounded will hold pride of place, Eucharist becomes the focus for the community's call and commitment to live in communion with all persons and to work for justice. All are invited to the table of the Lord. There is to be no hierarchical or discriminatory distinction of persons, as such distinctions are at odds with the one who is looked to in faith and hope at this table.

Eucharist is sharing of the most basic sort. Without the willingness to share at this most basic level, there can be no justice. Such sharing is a corporate statement of willingness to live a life of communion and justice, of solidarity in faith and service, together with those whom Jesus was not afraid or ashamed to call brothers and sisters.

Ethical Implications of Celebrating the Eucharist

As the central expression of the church's call and commitment to *communion* and *justice*, the Eucharist comprises the heart of a Christian morality. Divisions and failure to share signal a failure to discern the Body of the Lord. Unwillingness to share in life as well as in the Eucharist, self-preoccupation, self-absorption, and self-indulgence all constitute a failure to discern God's presence which is remembered and hoped for in the bread and the cup.

Those who share at the table of his remembrance enjoin themselves to live in accord with a covenant morality which stems from membership in God's people: to live according to the Spirit and not according to the flesh (Rom. 8).

The willingness of Christians to share extends beyond those gathered at the table, beyond the covenant community to all who constitute the human family, with particular attention to the poor and wounded—those whom Jesus promised will hold pride of place in the reign of God which is anticipated in the eucharistic meal.

As participation in a ritual meal of communion and justice, the Eucharist does not permit distinction of persons: divisions, separations, and distinction of persons based on race, class, sex, handicap, status, and rank are decried; a willingness is expressed to work toward the overcoming of such divisions, factions, and distinctions of persons so that Christ may be all in all (Gal. 3:27–28). To celebrate the Eucharist implies that we live our lives motivated by a vision of justice and communion. To break bread and share the cup is to live in the memory of his death, to have died with him. To have died with Christ is to live for God and for the coming of God's reign wherein the power of love prevails over all evil.

Pastoral Practice and Problems

The Eucharist is the heart of the Roman Catholic community, the source and summit of the life of faith. In eucharistic celebration the identity of the Christian community as the Body of Christ is given and received. If all of this is true, then more appropriate liturgical practice should be apparent in the life of the church.

Above all else, more attention needs to be given to the assembly as the primary symbol in any liturgical celebration. Often liturgy is viewed as the action of the priest alone. Although a variety of ministries may be exercised, such as reader, server, cantor, or deacon, the impression is often communicated that the Eucharist is something done by the one who presides—the presbyter or priest. Attention needs to be given to the ways in which all ministries, including that of presiding at liturgy (the role of presbyter), are ministries *from* the assembly and *to* the assembly. Such an understanding of liturgy as the act of a community requires suitable liturgical preparation and planning if we are to call forth and recognize many ministries. Without this fundamental change in thought and practice the liturgy stands little chance of being true to its own nature as a community's act of remembrance and thanksgiving.

The community's act of remembering is expressed not only in the breaking of the bread and sharing of the cup, but in the whole prayer of thanksgiving, the eucharistic prayer, which articulates that remembrance. More attention, then, must be paid to narrative and commemoration which provide the setting for the liturgical activity of breaking bread and sharing the cup. The central action of breaking and sharing may then be seen alongside the other images of Jesus as one who feeds the hungry and washes the feet of the followers as a servant. The focal symbolic action of breaking and sharing is thereby enriched through the narrative which places this action alongside other actions in the Scriptures which reveal the meaning and message of Jesus.

Finally, there is the singular significance of the proclamation and hearing of the word. Christian liturgy is an act of remembrance and of hope, and as these are expressed in worship and in the word, God's presence is discerned. The Eucharist is a celebration of God's presence not only in the actual sacramental actions of breaking bread and sharing the cup, but in the proclamation and hearing of the word as well. In practice eucharistic celebration often gives short shrift to the place of the word in liturgy, even though it now finds a more prominent place in the Roman liturgy. The liturgy is an act of worship which recognizes God's presence in both word and sacrament. Therefore greater attention must be given to proclamation and interpretation of the word, which thus necessitates a greater recognition of the indispensable ministries of teaching in the life of the church.

Notes

1. The revised rite of anointing, *Pastoral Care of the Sick: Rites of Anointing and Viaticum*, makes clear that anointing is the sacrament of the seriously ill and dying, and that Eucharist, viaticum, is the sacrament to be received at death's door. For a useful treatment of viaticum, see Charles Gusmer, *And You Visited Me: Sacramental Ministry to the Sick and Dying* (New York: Pueblo Publishing Co., 1984), p. 114ff.

2. See David N. Power, *The Sacrifice We Offer: The Tridentine Dogma and Its Reinterpretation* (New York: Crossroad Publishing Co., 1987).

3. Johann Baptist Metz, *Faith in History and Society* (New York: Crossroad Publishing Co., 1980), p. 88ff. Metz refers to the memory of Jesus as a "dangerous memory," one which unsettles and calls into question assumptions about the way things are and the way things ought to be.

4. See Monika Hellwig, *Jesus, The Compassion of God* (Wilmington, DE: Glazier, 1983). See also Leonardo Boff, *Jesus Christ Liberator* (Maryknoll, NY: Orbis, 1978).

5. This point is developed at length by Matthew Lamb, *Solidarity with Victims* (New York: Crossroad Publishing Co., 1982); and by Rebecca Chopp, *The Praxis of Suffering* (Maryknoll, NY: Orbis, 1986).

6. This understanding of church is developed at length by Leonardo Boff, *Church: Charism and Power* (New York: Crossroad Publishing Co., 1985), p. 8ff.

7. For an excellent, in-depth survey of the development of the Eucharist as sacrifice, see Power, *The Sacrifice We Offer*.

8. Faith and Order Commission of the World Council of Churches, paper no. 111, *Baptism, Eucharist and Ministry* (Geneva: World Council of Churches, 1982). See also *Catholic Perspectives on Baptism, Eucharist and Ministry*, ed. Michael Fahey (Lanham, MD: University Press of America, 1986).

9. The Greek term *anamnesis* does not signify simple recall. It describes the activity whereby, through remembrance, past events are rendered present.

10. For a superb treatment of the nature of lament, see Walter Brueggemann, "The Costly Loss of Lament," *Journal for the Study of the Old Testament* 36 (October 1986): 57–71. See also Claus Westermann, *Praise and Lament in the Psalms* (Atlanta: John Knox Press, 1981).

11. The Greek term *epiclesis* describes the invocation of the Spirit. Together with *anamnesis*, the *epiclesis* forms the heart of the eucharistic prayer of the church.

12. From the third eucharistic prayer of the Roman Missal.

6

Sacraments of Reconciliation and Healing

Most Roman Catholics would agree that, next to the Eucharist, no sacrament has undergone more change since the time of Vatican II than penance. The word associated with the sacrament of penance is *reconciliation*, which indicates the end of an approach marked by a heavy preoccupation with sinful acts.

The sacrament of anointing of the sick and dying has likewise undergone profound change. Previously referred to as "extreme unction," the sacrament was received only in the most dire circumstances, or on the deathbed. Today the sacrament is celebrated in remembrance of Christ's healing ministry, often in the company of family, friends, and community. Healing and support are focal, even if the illness or the suffering ends in death.

Both sacraments are properly understood from the perspective of reconciliation and healing necessitated by the effects of sin and evil in our world. The sacrament of penance focuses upon our need for reconciliation with God, conscience, and community because of our capitulation to evil which results in sin. The sacrament of anointing addresses our need for healing due to the effects of evil and sin upon the individual and the community.

This chapter will look at the history of the sacrament of penance with particular attention to those factors which might inform a contemporary understanding and practice of the sacrament. Consideration will be given to the *Rite of Penance* and what it offers to the present attempt to find appropriate forms of conversion and reconciliation.[1] We will then treat the question of the future of penance in light of the recognition that the church now stands at a new moment in a very complex historical process. Finally, what is said about the sacrament of penance will be more directly related to the healing and reconciling ministry of Jesus.

The sacrament of anointing will also be treated in this chapter within the broader context of the ministry to and pastoral care of the sick and dying. Particular attention will be given to the revised rite of anointing, which expresses a vision of anointing which is considerably different from the earlier practice of extreme unction.[2]

Historical Overview of the Sacrament of Penance

The history of the sacrament of penance is a story of the dynamics of reconciliation with God, conscience, and community through confession, repentance, and forgiveness. At any given historical period one or another element may come to the fore, but the same dynamics are operative: reconciliation through confessing of sin, doing penance, and receiving forgiveness. These are still found in our present practice of the sacrament.

Early Public Penance

In the early church there was clear acknowledgment that even the baptized sin daily and that constant conversion is necessary. There was not, however, a separate sacrament of penance as we know it. Persons dealt with sin by prayer, fasting, almsgiving, love of neighbor, Eucharist, and through the advice and guidance of holy persons. However, some grave sins demanded particular attention. These were sins that were understood to go against the very nature of the community and its faith, thereby disrupting its existence. Hence a practice of penance developed characterized by exclusion from the Lord's table, initiation to public penance, and the recognition of one's need for public reconciliation if one were to return to the Lord's table.

Because of the need for some to do public penance, this early practice of penance was also characterized by the constitution of an "order of penitents" marked by their garb of sackcloth and ashes. Aside from wearing distinctive clothing, the penitents were set off from the rest of the community by their place in church, the severity of their fast, and their taking up other disciplinary measures and acts of mortification.

During this early period, there were various attempts to list the sins that seriously ruptured links with the community and required public penance. Though universal agreement was not reached as to what constituted grave sin, the list would include heresy, adultery, murder, apostasy, schism, and the rape of virgins. All of these were understood to constitute an assault on the fundamental meanings and values of the community. For example, schism threatened the integrity, unity, and well-being of the community. The rape of virgins violated one of the fundamental values of the community, that of virginity—which during this period was laden with eschatological significance.

The breakdown of the practice of public penance resulted from several causes. First, because of the extension of the list of sins to include such matters as fornication, more people were required to do public penance. In practice, however, they were prevented from doing so. The longer the lists grew, the more this practice of penance was diverted from its original purpose. Second, the practice waned because of the general rule that reconciliation could be granted only once in a lifetime. Consequently, the young were dissuaded from entering the order of penitents until the passing of the vigor and passion of youth. Third, the practice of admission to the Eucharist of some not publicly reconciled began to emerge. More and more sinners sought reconciliation by means which bypassed public penance. Finally, anointing came to be used as deathbed reconciliation. Persons who had avoided public penance were reconciled at last. This practice encouraged others to delay their reconciliation and thereby avoid the discipline of public penance, which in many cases was very harsh.

The Rise of Private Penance

Beginning in the sixth and seventh centuries, penance began to take a very different form in continental Europe. This form finds strong roots in an Irish system of penance influenced by a monastic model of regular confession of faults to the abbot or spiritual guide. This penitential system was adapted to the needs of those on the Continent in nonmonastic as well as monastic settings. In such adaptation what was stressed was the contact between confessor and penitent. In this practice reconciliation was brought about privately and more than once in a lifetime. However, penance was still extended over a very long period of time, and reconciliation was granted only after the penance was completed.

The penitential books, which are associated with the Irish system and its adaptation to Continental needs, were meant as a help to confessors in guiding penitents through the process of conversion. The penitential books, which contained lists of sins with appropriate penances, were sometimes misused and resulted in a tit-for-tat legalistic approach to penance on the part of confessors and penitents.

From this practice developed a greater stress on the actual confession of sin as an act of humility and a gesture of repentance so that reconciliation might be granted sooner and penances lightened. This stress on the act of confession itself was intensified in the high Middle Ages, with its accent on the individual person's deeds, rather than on the actions of a community. The act of confessing was then explained as a humble submission of one's sins to the judgment of God together with the submission of the heart to the working of the grace of Christ.

Penances had become much lighter than those of the early public practice. They were performed *after* absolution, or the granting of forgiveness, and explained as making satisfaction for sin rather than as actions which lead to conversion, and which are themselves part of the conversion process itself.

This approach was strengthened by the definitions of the Council of Trent, which stressed the need for integral confession—the confession of all and every mortal sin. The approach was further consolidated by defining the role of the confessor as judge and minister of the grace of pardon.

Learning from History

From this brief overview of the history of the sacrament of penance several points of importance emerge for us today.

Conversion from sin is a process which is achieved over a period of time. The process entails a change of heart and of conduct, which is brought about by prayer, acts of charity, and deeds of mortification. Conversion requires a more intense participation in the Eucharist and in the life of the Christian community. It is assisted by guidance or spiritual direction. All conversion is achieved with the assistance of others in a community of Christian faith.

History shows that some sins are of such a nature that they make participation at the Lord's table impossible. In each age there has been an attempt to spell out what such sins are. Our own age is challenged with the same task, as we shall see later in this chapter.

In effecting reconciliation the bishop or priest is the minister of God and of the church. However, the history of the sacrament clearly indicates that others may provide some of the guidance and advice that people need on the way to conversion. For us today this has important consequences as Christians seek reconciliation in various ways, such as spiritual guidance, and pastoral counseling. The challenge is to relate such practices to the process of conversion, a vital dimension of which is the sacrament of penance.

History illustrates that each age has had need of a different system of integrating the elements of confession, repentance, forgiveness, and related elements within an overall vision and practice of Christian life. In our own day the new *Rite of Penance*, which resulted from the work of the Second Vatican Council and its commissions, is an attempt to find an appropriate form of conversion and reconciliation in light of the needs and urgent demands of our age.

Before turning to a consideration of the new *Rite of Penance*, let us give attention to those factors in the first half of the twentieth century which helped to shape an understanding of the human person, sin, and the nature of conversion and reconciliation, and which have, consequently, influenced the practice of the sacrament of penance.

Influences upon a Contemporary Understanding of Reconciliation

Vatican II is often described in terms of the monumental changes to which it gave rise. Perhaps it is more appropriate, however, to look at the council as a response to monumental changes which had already taken place in the world and in the church. The change in the ways of perceiving and being in the church may have been very subtle and unconscious to a certain degree, but significant changes had already been set in motion which were then given sanction and further impetus by the council.

Even prior to the council, pastors and theologians were beginning to find that the categories of the Middle Ages and subsequent ages were not always useful in addressing problems that confronted persons in the twentieth century.

In every area of theology there was a movement away from externalism and legalism. This is especially true of moral theology, which, among other things, looks at the nature of human acts and the ordering of human action to its proper end. Moral theology began to give increasing attention to developments in psychology and phenomenology, which, in one of its forms, focuses on the progressive development of mind. Judgments about right and wrong, good and bad, came to be viewed as no longer possible solely in terms of keeping or breaking the preestablished moral code. There was increasing awareness that sin and sinfulness must be considered and judged in light of internal decisions and motivations, not just on the basis of external actions.

In the domain of moral theology (or ethics) a key figure in Catholic thought and life during this period was Bernard Häring. In his monumental *The Law of Christ*,[3] he spells out some of the implications of these insights for Christian moral life and so for the sacrament of reconciliation. Informed by the breakthroughs in biblical scholarship then current, Häring's work recovers the insight that the basic moral category of the Bible is not law but covenant, which implies relationship, loving responsibility, and fidelity.

The work of Joseph Fuchs also contributed to the development of new understandings in moral theology. His focus upon the larger orientation of a life toward good or evil by a basic choice or fundamental option threw light on the truth that moral judgments about specific external actions can only be made when seen in light of this choice.[4]

The personalist philosophy of others such as Joseph Fletcher enabled confessors and theologians to take account of the interpersonal, relational factors in human decision and action.[5] Morality, for Fletcher, cannot be understood simply as personal adjustment to society's norms. Particular persons in very concrete situations need to be judged in light of the intentions, motivations, and personal relations at issue. According to Fletcher, the ultimate criterion for the judgment of actions is love, not adherence to preestablished norms.

All of these influences shaped the understanding of right and wrong, human decision and action, one's relationship to God, conscience, and community. Quite naturally, then, these influences had an impact upon the understanding of the sacrament of penance.

The two world wars, the events of Hiroshima and Nagasaki, and the dawning awareness of the question of civil rights brought to the fore the reality of "social sin." Although those at the council do not seem to have been directly concerned with the question of social sin vis-à-vis sacramental life, the renewal of the sacrament of penance which began during the 1960s gives evidence of an increased consciousness of social responsibility. It reflects a deeper awareness of the social as well as the personal nature of evil and sin. Faced with such realities as racism, classism, sexism, environmental pollution, and world hunger, Roman Catholics began to question how the practice of private penance was related to these much larger realities which are forms of evil and sin.

If the Second Vatican Council did little to change the theology of penance, it was, however, aware of the fact that the sacrament of penance had taken a variety of forms to meet the needs of various epochs. Such awareness was due, in large part, to the contributions of church historians. The bishops of the council recognized that if the practice of penance had changed in the past, it could change again.

The New Rite of Penance

Aware of the changes which were occurring on the contemporary scene, and looking at earlier practices of penance in the Western as well as Eastern Christian churches, church leaders charged a liturgical committee with the work of revising the ritual of penance. The aim was to revise the rite in such a way that it would be less individualistic and more communal, less legalistic and more liturgical, with less focus on enumeration of sins and more on conversion. The rite stresses mercy, conversion, and reconciliation with church and with God, because sin offends the church, the body of believers, as well as God.

The new *Rite of Penance* was released in 1973 and officially replaced the rite then in use. Three major concerns are found in the revised rite. First, great attention is given to the necessity of conversion, rather than only to confession of sins. Not merely a conversion of conduct is envisioned, but a real change of heart. The new rite views conversion or contrition as *a new way of looking at one's life.*[6] The perspective from which it is to be seen is that of God's holiness and mercy. As a result, the sacrament of penance is not a place of judgment where punishment is given or stern reprimand delivered. It is not the place for demanding satisfaction. Rather, the sacrament is an action that offers God's mercy and forgiveness; it is to guide the penitent to discover those acts and insights which will direct her or him to a real change of heart, which entails a reorientation of intention and action toward the good.

Second, prominence is given to the role which God's word plays in conversion. God's word calls to repentance, offers forgiveness, aids in converting the heart, and points to the true nature of sin and of conversion. Hence the rite strongly recommends the use of Scripture in addition to the prescribed prayers: here again the influence of word in worship and sacrament is brought to the fore.

Third, it is clear that the rite is an attempt to find a way of meeting the needs of individual persons and of celebrating penance as a community sacrament at one and the same time. Here the impact of the growing awareness of the corporate or social dimension of sin and sinfulness is clearly seen. Human sin is not only an individual, personal act. Not a purely private matter, it has corporate, social causes and consequences as well.

The new *Rite of Penance* provides a system particular to our age, and is an expression of the church's attempt to deal with the reality of sin and the presence of sinners.

Three Distinct Rites

The new *Rite of Penance* is still in the process of implementation and adaptation to local circumstances and needs. What the revised rite provides are three distinct rites of penance.

The first is a rite for individual penance, a one-to-one encounter between priest and penitent. This includes a face-to-face option, thereby making the confessional screen, required in earlier practice, optional. The rite should be a real celebration, where both priest and penitent listen to God's word and look together at the penitent's life. It should be the occasion for the expression of sorrow and hope through appropriate forms of prayer. The priest pronounces pardon and reconciliation in God's name and in the name of the whole church. Both priest and penitent express thanksgiving.

The second rite is a communal celebration of penance into which individual confession is inserted. Public proclamation of God's word, a common examination of conscience, and a common act of thanksgiving are accented. Perhaps the only disadvantage of this rite is that it allows little space for individual guidance.

The advantages of the second rite far outweigh whatever disadvantages there might be. A major advantage is that at appropriate times of the year, for example, Lent, Advent, before occasions of baptism, confirmation, or parish feast, it allows people to see their own sin and need for conversion within a corporate, communal context. It also allows the community to recognize the corporate nature of human sin.

Some pastors and communities actually prefer to have penitential services of the word without individual confession. Individual confession is provided for at other times, but within a larger parish project related to the service of the word. For example, all of those who intend to make confession of their sins during Lent are invited to one penitential service of the word at the beginning of the season, and to another service of thanksgiving at the end.

The third is a rite of general absolution, provided for what are seen as rare occasions. Such rare occasions would include those in which the number of penitents grossly exceeds the resources of available confessors. When this rite is used, the discipline still insists on the need for individual confession.

Some have come to feel that the occasions for general absolution are far more frequent than the rite allows, and that the need for individual confession is given much too legal an emphasis, instead of being placed within the proper context of the need for personal guidance on the path to conversion of heart and of conduct.

The various rites of penance throughout history reflect the richness and diversity of sacramental reconciliation. Each epoch has had its own form, more or less appropriate to the age. The three distinct rites of the new *Rite of Penance* are attempts to respond to the needs of the present age. But the present age is one of crisis: a crisis of vision and of hope. Is the new rite, even with its variety of forms, appropriate for today? In light of the changes which have shaped our understanding of the human person and the human community, particularly in light of the reality of social sin, it must be asked if the new *Rite of Penance* is an effective means of reconciliation with God, conscience, and community. Whatever the final judgment may be, it is crucial to recognize that our own age is a new moment in a complex historical development of the way the church deals with the reality of sin and the presence of sinners.

The Future of the Sacrament of Penance

Some theologians and pastors would suggest that the new *Rite of Penance* came too late, and that people had long since questioned and decided issues of sin and morality on their own. Others maintain that in North America and Western Europe the issue of birth control led an enormous number of people to question the nature and necessity of confession. Many who continued to go to confession stopped confessing the use of artificial contraceptives because they did not see it as sinful. As a result, the image of priest as final arbiter in matters of morality came to be questioned. Individuals stressed personal responsibility, freedom, and conscience. In serious matters, professional counselors came to be consulted instead of priests.

In the years between the Second Vatican Council and the appearance of the *Rite of Penance* in 1973, the practice of penance then in use broke down, and it appears that the new forms have not taken its place. Some pastors and theologians speculate that the future practice of penance will be much like its very early past when sacramental reconciliation was sought rarely, if ever. Others suggest that if penance is to be adequately sacramental, more focus must be placed on the communal celebration of penance, which has greater potential for highlighting a community's sinfulness and a deeper awareness of the social nature of sin, not just the personal.

The future of sacramental reconciliation has roots in the past, and these we have glimpsed in our historical survey. But its future also has roots in present practice. A look at two factors on the contemporary scene may enable us to discern the contours of the future shape of the sacrament of penance.

First, there is an ongoing shift in understanding what sin is. Although some would argue forcefully that people today have no sense of sin, it would be more accurate to say that people have not lost a sense of sin, but are unable to articulate it. We have learned from the brief historical survey of the sacrament of penance that each age has tried to list, or spell out, what sins make participation at the Lord's table impossible. People today have a profound sense of sin, but the problem and the challenge lie in "naming" sin. In our own day focus is not so exclusively and narrowly upon the sexual as the domain of sin. The focus is more and more upon the area of justice, human rights, mercy and compassion, and the ways in which sin and evil thwart the coming of God's reign of justice, truth, unity, mercy, and peace. Sacramental reconciliation must help the Christian community to articulate its sense of sin, to name it, and to bring it before God's face. The future of the sacrament of penance rests upon its ability to respond to the different needs of the age, and to continually enable persons and communities to spell out their sense of the sinful and their need for forgiveness. Thus the future of the sacrament need not be similar to its early past, but may take new and seemingly unprecedented paths as the Christian community finds itself again and again in need of reconciliation.

A second factor on the contemporary scene is the rise of different ways by which people seek reconciliation with God, conscience, and community. While the practice of the sacrament of penance appears to be on the decline, the growth in the area of spiritual direction, spiritual advising and counseling, retreats, and the like is astounding. Our historical survey has shown that all conversion is achieved with the help of others in a Christian community. The ministries of spiritual direction, pastoral counseling and advising must be recognized as services which provide some of the guidance and advice that people need on the way to conversion, while recognizing the bishop or priest as the minister of God and the church in effecting sacramental reconciliation. All these activities are built upon a one-to-one relationship which is ongoing. The director, adviser, or counselor is often a noncleric. She or he is sought out on the basis of the spiritual gifts manifested in her or his life, not on the basis of the office conferred. Although not sacramental in the restricted sense, such practices are viewed by directors and directees alike as occasions of God's healing and reconciliation. Such practices find root and precedent in the practice of the early Irish church wherein the *anamchara*, or soul friend, often a noncleric, was sought out for the insight and wisdom offered.[7]

The practice of alternative expressions of healing and reconciliation, together with the increasing involvement of the nonordained in this ministry, are shaping the future of the sacrament of penance. If the private, one-to-one form of the rite is to be truly sacramental in the church of the future, then its dynamics must be situated within a much broader context of reconciliation and healing, and within a prolonged process involving extended one-to-one contact.

Finally, the future practice of the sacrament of penance needs to emphasize ever more clearly the nature of the sacrament of penance as an offering of God's forgiveness, rather than as a rendering of divine judgment, as the church finds itself again and again in need of God's forgiveness in the future.

Penance: Rooted in Jesus' Ministry of Reconciliation

Our attention has focused primarily upon the various ways in which the church attempts to deal with the reality of sin and the presence of sinners. The sacramental ritual of penance has been to the fore; however, it must not be overlooked that the various sacramental rites of penance, present as well as past, give form to the ministry of reconciliation entrusted to the whole church. Hence the sacrament of penance must be seen as rooted in an ecclesiological base. The church is itself sacrament of forgiveness and reconciliation. Likewise, in accord with principles articulated in the second chapter of this book, the sacrament of penance is rooted in the ministry of Jesus Christ, who is primordial sacrament of God's forgiveness and reconciliation. In brief, the sacrament of penance is an expression of the church as sacrament of reconciliation which is the continuing and meaningful expression of the forgiving and reconciling love of God made manifest in Christ Jesus.

To speak of the sacrament of penance as rooted in Jesus Christ is not to propose a narrow view of institution which views the establishment of the sacrament of penance, as we know it, in miniature. Difficulties with such an approach to institution have been pointed out before (chap. 2). It is rather to suggest that the sacrament of penance has emerged in different forms, more or less appropriate to various epochs, as the church has struggled to remember the ministry of Jesus to sinners. For it was sinners he came to heal, not the perfect and self-righteous (Matt. 9:10–13). Forgiveness and reconciliation are central to the message of Jesus and essential for entry into God's reign. Hence the singular significance of Jesus' call to repentance and belief. The nearness of the reign of God which he preached entailed repentance for sin, as well as a promise of forgiveness. The message which he proclaimed posed an ethical challenge to those who heard it: to live from the perspective of God's forgiveness and mercy not only for oneself but for all people. God's mercy knows no bounds. It is showered upon the evil as well as the good, the dishonest as well as the honest (Matt. 5:43–48).

Since God's presence draws near in Jesus, the life and ministry of Jesus manifests God's own reconciling and forgiving love. Jesus is close to sinners, yet distant from the self-righteous. His parables promise forgiveness. They probe and call into question the validity of human judgments. Perhaps the finest example of such a view of forgiveness and reconciliation is the parable of the prodigal son (Luke 15:11–32). This parable holds out a vision of conversion and of life transformed by the knowledge of God's mercy, which breaks the boundaries of sin as well as the categories of human judgment. It best expresses the dynamic of Christian life lived in the consciousness of sin and grace. Although we may strive to search our own conscience, come to know our motivation in doing the good that we do, overcome our failings and faults, and give ourselves over to the process of conversion of heart and conduct, in the final analysis we come up against our own sinfulness and are totally dependent upon the forgiveness and reconciliation that come from God alone. This parable expresses what is the essence of Christian liturgy and sacrament in general, and sacramental reconciliation in particular: God's promise is an offer of unrestricted forgiveness; a healing and reconciliation beyond what we dare ask, deserve, or imagine. Where sin abounds, grace abounds even more.

Perhaps one may find it strange that such a lengthy treatment is given to the sacrament of penance. But recall that our primary purpose is to treat the relationship between sacraments and morality, liturgy and life. Christian morality has to do with realizing, making real in our lives, the original gift of grace and Spirit given in the sacraments of initiation in the way we live and act. The sacrament of penance expresses our continuing need for forgiveness because we as persons and communities neglect or betray that gift. In celebrating this sacrament we live out of a new vision of reality, from the perspective of God's mercy and forgiveness, so that yet again we can take up the task of assisting the coming of the reign of God which is anticipated at the table of the Lord.

The Sacrament of Anointing and Pastoral Care of the Sick

The practice of anointing the sick and dying is rooted in the healing ministry of Jesus and in the church's care of the sick from the earliest days of its life (James 5:14–16). Like the sacrament of penance, the sacrament of anointing has taken a variety of forms throughout the ages in response to varying needs and different ways of perceiving life and being in the world. The revised rite of anointing of the sick is an attempt to address present needs and reflects a vision of the healing ministry of the church as it struggles against illness, suffering, and depersonalization.

Earlier practices of this sacrament did not always keep to the fore the notion of healing, which is the raison d'être of the sacrament. *Healing* is a term often misunderstood, however. When used in description of the purpose of anointing, it is not to be understood primarily as miraculous intervention into the life of the sick or dying person. The rationale for the sacrament is twofold. First, in anointing, the church offers its support and what it might contribute to recovery and health. Second, anointing is intended to bring spiritual strength to sustain the person in her or his illness with a hope in the Resurrection, even if the sickness should lead to death. It is understood as sacrament of healing in that it offers strength, support, and sustenance.

The revised rite follows the directives of the Second Vatican Council's *Constitution on the Sacred Liturgy*. The Latin text of the rite was released by the Congregation for Divine Worship on 7 December 1972. It was to be universally implemented by 1 January 1974. In accord with the terms of the council, the revised and updated rite of anointing is treated within the context of pastoral ministry to the sick. That is to say, the community's care for the seriously ill and dying frames the sacramental experience of anointing.

The new rite highlights anointing as sacrament of the sick. It is no longer seen as the sacrament of death. The terms *extreme unction* and *last rites* have been avoided. The title of the rite and the arrangement of its chapters indicate the focus upon the importance of the ministry to the sick. There is a clearer distinction between pastoral care of the sick and pastoral care of the dying, with viaticum, or Eucharist as food for the passage through death to eternal life, emerging as the sacrament proper to the dying.[8]

The essential rite of the sacrament of anointing consists of anointing those who are seriously ill due to sickness or old age. The translation of the Latin *periculose aegrotans* as "seriously" rather than "gravely" or "dangerously" or "perilously ill" is meant to avoid unnecessary restriction of the sacrament.[9] Forehead and hands are anointed with blessed olive oil or, according to circumstances and custom, another plant oil. While anointing, the priest says, "Through this holy anointing may the Lord in his love and mercy help you with the grace of the Holy Spirit. . . . May the Lord who frees you from sin save you and raise you up" (no. 25).[10]

The rite departs from the previous practice on several points. No longer are the five senses anointed, only the forehead and hands. No longer is the danger of death a condition for anointing. In line with what is said in the Letter of James 5:14–16, those whose health is seriously impaired by sickness or old age are the recipients of the sacrament. The sacrament is to be administered as early as possible in the course of serious illness. The anointing may be repeated in the course of the same illness if the condition of the sick person worsens.

It is crucial to see that anointing is understood within the context of pastoral ministry to the sick. The new rite provides a pastoral and theological rationale for anointing which views it as part of the church's struggle to overcome suffering and illness. Where they are not overcome they can bear positive significance through participation in the mystery of the cross and Resurrection of Christ.

Ministries to the sick are seen within a very broad perspective. Ministry to the sick is viewed as the responsibility of all men and women who serve the sick in any capacity. All baptized Christians are responsible for ministering to the sick, although the specific responsibilities differ according to the gifts given to each individual. Particular focus is upon the family and friends of the sick person and the priest who is the proper minister of the sacrament of anointing. Visiting and caring for the sick is not simply the responsibility of priests; it is the mission of the entire Christian community.

The ecclesial context for the ministry and anointing of the sick is clearly reflected in the movement from the earlier practice of private, final anointings as normative to the possibility of a communal service within a liturgical setting involving community, family, and friends—as well as for the anointing of several persons at once. Group anointings may take place within the eucharistic liturgy after the proclamation of the word as a distinct ritual for the sole purpose of anointing or within the context of a communion service.

A large-scale effort is necessary to correct earlier misunderstandings of the sacrament as exclusively for the dying, or more particularly, for those at death's door. The new rite more clearly expresses the purposes of the sacrament of anointing and pastoral ministry to the sick: to offer the church's support and what it might lend to recovery and health; to strengthen the spirit to sustain the person with hope in the Resurrection, even if illness leads to death.

Ethical Implications of the Sacraments of Reconciliation and Healing

Our purpose is not to prescribe codes of Christian conduct, but it is still possible to provide the particular contours of the moral horizon expressed in the celebration of the sacraments of reconciliation and healing. In celebrating the sacrament of penance Christians express a new vision of reality. They live within the perspective of God's *mercy* and *forgiveness*. The Lordship of Jesus Christ and the empowerment of the Holy Spirit are the criteria by which judgments and decisions are made about ourselves and others. Compassion is the ethical hallmark here. Judgments about one's own life and the lives of others are made in light of a consciousness of sin and grace in the events of human life. As a result, the lives of the rejected and the scorned, the outcast and the forgotten, those judged to be worthless and waste by the criteria of efficiency, productivity, and propriety, come to be seen from the perspective of God's mercy and forgiveness. In light of the consciousness of sin and grace, the wounded, the weak, the little, the fragile, and poor are viewed as disclosing God's grace and mercy, which touches them in the greatness of their need. Hidden in the lives of those who are poor and wounded, and in our own poverty and frailty, are found the seeds of God's promise of mercy and forgiveness. Those who respond to God's love and attraction become the clearest signs of God's reconciling love in our world. Life itself becomes an echo of the testament of Paul: in our weakness is God's strength (2 Cor. 12:9–10).

Through the sacrament of anointing the Christian community lives in remembrance of Christ's healing ministry. As such, Christians are called upon to *care* for the sick, to *struggle against illness, suffering,* and *depersonalization.* In celebrating the sacrament of anointing, the community expresses a new perspective on suffering, illness, and death which enables Christians to live in the hope and with the confidence that nothing escapes the grasp of God's healing and compassion in Jesus Christ.

Notes

1. The *Rite of Penance* first appeared as *Ordo Paenitentiae* (2 December 1973). See *The Rites of the Catholic Church* (New York: Pueblo Publishing Co., 1976), p. 337ff. For a thorough treatment of penance, see James Dallen, *The Reconciling Community: The Rite of Penance* (New York: Pueblo Publishing Co., 1986).

2. The *Rite of Anointing and Pastoral Care of the Sick* appeared as the translation of *Ordo Unctionis Infirmorum Eorumque Pastoralis Curae* (7 December 1972). See *The Rites of the Catholic Church*, p. 573ff. The original has been translated, revised, and published as *Pastoral Care of the Sick: Rites of Anointing and Viaticum* (Washington, DC: ICEL, 1982).

3. This has been revised and updated under the title *Free and Faithful in Christ*, 3 vols. (New York: Crossroad Publishing Co., 1978–81).

4. Joseph Fuchs, *Human Values and Christian Morality* (Dublin: Gill and Macmillan, 1970), chap. 4, "Basic Freedom and Morality."

5. Joseph Fletcher, *Situation Ethics* (Philadelphia: Westminster Press, 1966).

6. The *Rite of Penance*, no. 6.

7. Pádraig Ó Fiannachta, "The Spirituality of the Céili Dé," *Irish Spirituality*, ed. Michael Maher (Dublin: Veritas, 1981), pp. 22–32. See p. 27ff.

8. Charles Gusmer, *And You Visited Me: Sacramental Ministry to the Sick and Dying* (New York: Pueblo Publishing Co., 1984), pp. ix–xv; see also p. 114ff. I am particularly indebted to Charles Gusmer's work for this treatment of anointing and pastoral care of the sick.

9. Ibid., p. 82.

10. Ibid., p. 70.

7

Being and Building the Body of Christ: Marriage, Ministries, Orders

Both marriage and orders are sacraments which express different ways of being and building the Body of Christ.[1] Both are services, ministries, by which the church is built, strengthened, and unified, and thereby God is glorified. Hence the larger context for treating both marriage and orders is that of ministry.

In Christian marriage, a community of two persons in love is at the service of the community which is the church. The call to Christian marriage is a personal one received from Christ and the Spirit in, through, and for the community which is the church. Children born of Christian marriage are the fruit of a community of love and also the invitation to a more inclusive communion of faith and love. Our approach to Christian marriage will be to look at five points.

First, we will look at the paradoxical and quite complex situation of contemporary relationships between man and woman. On the one hand, the contemporary scene is marked by an increased awareness of the importance of what marriage offers and demands. On the other, it seems that there has never been a time in history when marriage has undergone such a massive breakdown. Next, we shall turn attention to an understanding of Christian marriage as it developed over the centuries, with particular focus upon the image of the union between Christ and church as prototype of the marriage between Christians. Such an image, if properly understood, can be seen as an influential factor which has served to deepen the mutuality between man and woman in marriage. Then we shall look briefly at how marriage came to be understood as a Christian sacrament. We shall then spell out a Christian understanding of marriage, attentive to those elements which constitute it as a sacramental reality.

Finally, we shall look to the problems of practice and some pastoral concerns which arise in light of the large-scale breakdown of marriage in our age. Attention will be given to the various ways in which the church attempts to uphold the value of the integrity of marriage, to strengthen the awareness and sense of responsibility of Christian couples regarding the dignity and holiness of their sacramental union, while at the same time responding appropriately to the pastoral needs of those whose marriages have broken down.

Orders, or holy orders, will be treated within the larger context of ministry to community. This will necessitate a description of the notion of ministry based upon the New Testament. New forms and expressions of service in Christ's name characteristic of the present age will be looked at in light of a fresh understanding of ministry.

Since an understanding of ministry derives from an understanding of church, the renewed ecclesiology which has developed since the Second Vatican Council calls for a renewed vision of ministry. The understanding of ministry which derives from this renewed ecclesiology is based upon the image of Christ the servant. All ministries thus need to be related to the notion of service, not power or authority. The uniqueness of the ministry of the ordained will be looked to in terms of the service of unity, catholicity, and apostolicity in light of the ordained minister's role of presiding at the table of the Lord. Because this understanding of ministry results in significant changes in church life and practice, we will look at the tensions and transitions which are occurring now regarding the church's ministry. Finally, we will spell out some of the ethical implications of marriage and ministry.

Christian Marriage

Though Catholic teaching has insisted on its intrinsic value and worth, Christian marriage is often shortchanged when compared to the priesthood and consecrated religious life in the Catholic tradition. Marriage is a sacrament. It is second to none as a way of being and building the Body of Christ.

Present Paradox

Today, perhaps more than ever before, people have a profound appreciation for the union between man and woman. Strange though this may seem, it is quite true. Our own very limited perspective often blinds us to the strengths and weaknesses of previous ages. It was not always the case that the union of man and woman was looked upon or spoken of in terms of pleasure, love, and happiness. In different cultures and societies, at different historical periods, marriage was often held in little regard, and valued largely for its usefulness rather than as a good in itself.

In our own day deeper appreciation of the personal and sexual dimensions of the union between man and woman have gone into shaping a very different view of marriage. This is due in large measure to the significance attached to the dignity and value of each human person, which is one of the hallmarks of our own age—whether that dignity is always respected in practice or not.

A contemporary view of the union between man and woman places great emphasis upon the notions of pleasure, love, sexuality, responsibility, and happiness. Yet paradoxically, so few marriages seem to realize or attain what marriage is understood to offer. Perhaps because too much is expected of marriage, so many break down. Some would argue that marriage as it is projected and imagined in our own culture is so unreal and unrealizable that new marriages are bound to fail. Others suggest that a contemporary approach to the union between man and woman has become focused in a rather singular way upon the sexual to the detriment of the other essential elements of union. The singular focus upon sex has led persons in our own time to place exceedingly high demands upon human relationships, which then results in a series of monogamous relationships instead of lifelong union between husband and wife.

However marriage is viewed, it is clear that its present situation is paradoxical. That which people seem most desirous of—personal, sexual fulfillment in a relationship of intimacy—seems to be that which they seem unable to find and keep. When such a relationship of lifelong union between man and woman is found, inclusive of the dimensions of personal and sexual intimacy, it is perhaps the clearest sign of God's love and fidelity in our world. In this sense marriage can be looked to as basic human sacrament. It is for many people the first and foremost manifestation of a loving, faithful, personal God.[2]

Marriage in the New Testament

The period of the early church was one of patriarchal domination. The male was understood to be superior to the female. This understanding colored the way in which relationships were engaged in, communities structured, and societies governed. Needless to say, this was the presupposition at the base of marriage in both theory and practice. The man was understood as head of house, the woman vastly unequal to him. Mutuality was not a desirable element in relationships between woman and man in general, or in marriage in particular.

Christianity originated in a setting no less patriarchal. Yet we see in the life and ministry of Jesus extraordinary attention to the women around him, and a deep awareness of the value and dignity of their sex.[3] In accord with the whole pattern of his life and ministry, Jesus held in pride of place those whom the society of his day viewed as virtual nonpersons, those with no rights whatever: women and children among others. The prohibition against divorce (Matt. 19:1–9; Luke 16:18) is not simply a defense of marriage in the abstract or ideal sense, but a defense of woman who, according to the law of her day, could be divorced by her husband without being consulted. The law forbade her the right to divorce her husband under any circumstances, or to appeal.

The understanding of marriage expressed in Ephesians 5:21–33 has been used rather constantly in support of male superiority: as is often the case, the parts of this passage which suit the tastes of the reader have been emphasized. As a result, this passage and its interpretation have been used in support of the submission of woman to man and her obedience to him in all things. Yet this is not the only side of the message in the passage under consideration. What needs to be heard with equal force, and what has not been heard in the reading of this passage, is Paul's exhortation to the husband to be like Christ in self-sacrificing love. This letter thus provides a fundamental assault on machismo. The husband is exhorted to be like Christ and love his wife as Christ loves the church, the people. This love is not a love which dominates, but which serves. The husband is to be the servant of the wife. It is a love which frees, not oppresses. Thus the very passage of the New Testament which has been used in support of patriarchal domination and control in fact, on fresh reading in proper context, provides the basis for undercutting male domination and its consequences in every sphere of life.

The Union Between Christ and Church

It is true that Christianity has been influenced by patriarchy and male bias; however, the reverence for the dignity of woman and marriage which is seen in the life and ministry of Jesus, as well as in Paul's exhortation that the husband should love the wife as Christ loves the church, has contributed to understanding marriage as a relationship of mutuality. The notion of the union between Christ and church as the basis for understanding union between husband and wife has a long history, and is a prototype for the dealings between the sexes, particularly in marriage. Again, a fresh reading of the Scriptures enables us to see that emphasis needs to be placed upon the self-sacrificing love required of the husband who is to love his wife as Christ loves the church. Self-sacrificing love is also required of the wife, as is obedience and submission of the husband to the wife. Marriage "in the Lord," even from earliest times in the church, has been viewed as different from marriage in and of itself. The image of the union between Christ and church has enabled couples to live out the deeper implications of marriage, which, even in purely secular terms, demands self-sacrifice, obedience, and submission of both, not just one to the other.

Development of a Theology of Marriage

The early church had no ritual of Christian marriage. In the first nine or ten centuries of the church's life, marriage was not viewed as a sacrament, in the strict sense of the term. Marriage of Christians was, however, understood to be "in the Lord," and to reflect the union of Christ and church and the love of the Lord. It was out of this perception of marriage in the Lord that their love for one another and for others was understood to flow. The development of the theology of marriage as sacrament derived from this.

The theology of marriage developed slowly and gradually. Already in Augustine we see the contours of a theology of Christian marriage which has influenced the whole course of the church's approach to marriage. First of all, Augustine recognized the difference between the marriage of Christians and marriage in general. He understood marriage on the basis of sexual union and friendship. The sexual union between man and woman is based upon their fidelity to one another, which is at once a mirror of the fidelity of God and the context within which children are born and reared. The contemporary reader often finds little appeal in Augustine's style, approach, and negative view of sexuality. Be that as it may, the importance he gives to friendship, to sexuality as the basis for union, and to fidelity as the mirror of divine love and basis for procreation go together to comprise a solid understanding of what Christian marriage offers and demands.

This understanding of marriage in the Lord strengthened the sense of Christian marriage as different from marriage in and of itself. Because the union came to be understood as a sacred reality, couples and pastors began to feel the need to protect Christian marriage. It was this quite concrete need at the practical level, together with an increasing appreciation for the sacramentality of Christian marriage at the theoretical level, that led to the practice of church celebrations of Christian marriage.

This increased awareness of the sacramentality of marriage in practice and theory led the theologians of the eleventh century to formulate a theology of marriage. This theology was developed based upon the awareness of the sacramentality of the union between man and woman in the Lord, which mirrors both God's fidelity and the union between Christ and church. But this theology was also based on an appreciation of the sacramentality of the ritual of marriage; a ritual which had developed in response to the desire to protect and foster Christian marriage. In brief, the theology of Christian marriage which was developed during this period, and which comes to us in our own day, focuses primarily upon the union of man and woman in the Lord as sacramental *in and of its own nature*, but it also views the ritual celebration of this union in the presence of the church as a sacramental act.[4]

A Contemporary Theology of Marriage

Because marriage in the Lord is understood as sacramental in and of itself, the couple is, and has always been, viewed as the minister of the sacrament. At the same time, because marriage in the Lord is never a purely personal matter, it is ritualized in the presence of the community in word and sacrament. The ritual itself is a sacramental act, a public act done *in* the church, *before* the church, and *for* the church. Such an act, a public act in the presence of the community, may be quite difficult for those who have grown up in the "me generation." Yet Christian marriage, marriage in the Lord, is an act of commitment to one another *and to the Body which is the church*. It is a way of being and building the Body of Christ. Ideally it enables each partner to love, not only one another and whatever children may be born of their union, but the larger Christian and human communities as well. It is a participation in the self-sacrifice of Jesus expressed in the notion of the union between Christ and the church. It is thereby ministry to the community and a manifestation of the personal love and fidelity of God in the human and Christian communities.

A contemporary theology of marriage draws upon the richness of the tradition. It is based upon sexual union and an appreciation of sexuality, pleasure, and the dignity of the human person. An authentic view of Christian marriage does not view pleasure, personal fulfillment, and sexuality as secondary or incidental, but as elements which comprise the very meaning of marriage. Personal and sexual pleasure provides the very basis for the faithful union which mirrors the fidelity of God and provides the context within which children are born and reared.

Contemporary approaches to Christian marriage look upon the union more in terms of mutuality than in previous periods. This is well supported by a proper reading of Ephesians 5:21–33 and, above all else, by the creation account in Genesis which envisions the equality and mutuality of man and woman from the dawn of creation (Gen. 1:27).[5] The rich tradition of Christian marriage, laden with biblical images such as those mentioned above, provides opportunity, not obstacle, for moving toward a deeper sense of mutuality and equality of man and woman in marriage.

Although Christian marriage has largely been understood in terms of sexual union and fidelity viewed on that basis, fidelity to spouse is inclusive of much more than matters of sexual behavior. Fidelity to one's spouse has been and continues to be thought of in terms of conjugal fidelity—faithfulness in sexual matters is certainly the concrete expression and realization of faithfulness to one's spouse—but conjugal fidelity is not identical with the deeper sense of fidelity to which one is called in Christian marriage. It may happen that one never violates the sexual fidelity pledged in marriage, but at the same time never enters with one's spouse into a deep sense of fidelity, loyalty, confidence, and trust at the level of affectivity and deep intimacy. In brief, sexual fidelity is the *symbol* of a much deeper fidelity of the person: it does not guarantee it.

Children: Fruition of Love and Invitation to Love

Theologies of Christian marriage, past and present, place great emphasis on the importance of the bearing and rearing of children as one of the goods of marriage.[6] Children are viewed as fruit or expression of the community of love between man and woman. At the same time, children born of faithful sexual union offer an invitation to the couple, and to the church, to a more inclusive love. Here again, the self-sacrificial character of Christian marriage expressed in the image of the union between Christ and church comes to the fore. The man and woman are invited to give of themselves, not only to one another, and to the human and Christian communities, but quite concretely they are called to lay down their lives in service of the new life born of their union.

Theologies of Christian marriage likewise stress the importance of deep friendship, mutuality, and fidelity as the context within which the child grows. Good home and Christian family have always been viewed as essential to personal growth and development in Christian faith.

If, to some, the prohibition against divorce in the Roman Catholic church seems exceedingly harsh, and if prohibition against artificial contraception and abortion seems out of step with present needs and modes of living, it may be helpful to understand the deeper meanings which such legislation aims to protect. Prohibition against divorce is meant to uphold the value of the integrity of the union in faithful love between man and woman. The prohibition against artificial contraception and abortion, which in our own day must be recognized as two separate issues, is meant to uphold the dignity and value of human life, as well as the importance of children as fruition of the communion of love and invitation to a more inclusive and self-sacrificial love.

Pastoral Problems and Practices

As mentioned at the outset, marriage is quite a paradoxical reality at present. The intimacy of relationship, the faithful dedication, the sexual pleasure and union, and the communion of persons in love which marriage offers are so rarely achieved in our own day. That which people want most appears to be that for which they do not seem capable. Commitments are hard to make. Legislation allows for them to be easily broken, though the effects of such breaking may take years, even a lifetime, to heal. Sometimes one never really recovers from the breakdown of a marriage. Our society does not support commitment and fidelity in sexual matters or in other areas for that matter. In fact our society works against such fidelity. Children are viewed as not only undesirable but, at times, dispensable.

Such factors as these have gone to shape the state of marriage in our day and have contributed to its breakdown. The contemporary church is faced with the questions of divorce and remarriage, the nature of commitment, and questions of family planning. The church through its ministry has attempted to reach out in compassion to those with broken marriages through the various organizations which attempt to address the pastoral needs of the divorced and remarried. Recognizing the problems which young couples face, more attention has been given to preparation for marriage in such movements as the Cana Conference and Engaged Encounter, and to the sustaining of marriage, through such groups as Marriage Encounter.

All these illustrate the church's attempt to address new issues, while at the same time striving to maintain the value of the integrity of the union between man and woman. Whether or not such attempts are meeting the needs and demands of our age is another question.

In our own day perhaps one of the greatest needs in the life of the church is the ministry of marriage counselor. More attention needs to be given to the wealth of experience and knowledge which married persons have to offer married couples as they face critical or crucial moments in their marriage. Who is more likely to know the reality of marriage "from the inside out" than married couples themselves? Such persons might be trained so as to deepen this knowledge and make it available to others. This ministry would then need to be recognized as a gift for the service of the community, for the strengthening and building of the Body of Christ. It would then find its place alongside the other ministries which the Spirit encourages and calls forth in the life of the church of the present, for its health and growth in the future.

Ministry to Community

Vatican II drew upon the insights of theologians who, in the preceding decades, had contributed to a renewed understanding of the word *ministry*. Since the council there has been a further recovery of the New Testament understanding of *gift* and *service*. Such a recovery has fostered the dawning awareness of the plurality of ministries and of their significance for the life of the church.

Vatican II: Recovering Roots

Ministry means service. Latin versions of the Bible use the word *ministerium* to translate what in New Testament Greek is called *diakonia* and *liturgia*. *Diakonia* describes those activities in the church which arise from the empowerment by the Holy Spirit for the building up of the community of faith. The use of the term *liturgia* suggests that these activities are expressions of true worship, since in the building of the Body of Christ, God is honored and praised.

In its ecclesiastical usage, *ministerium* came to connote power and authority, which the New Testament terms *diakonia* and *liturgia* do not; the restriction of its usage to the ordained indicated the growing tendency to reduce the nonordained to a passive role, and to restrict ministry itself and responsibility almost exclusively to the ordained.

Vatican II did a great deal to reverse this tendency to confine ministry and responsibility to the ordained. In so doing, it contributed to a growing awareness of the indispensability of the active role of the laity in the overall mission of the church. This role had been evident in previous decades, especially in France.[7]

In its documents the council restricts the use of the language of ministry to the activities of the ordained, while using the terms *charisma*, *apostolatus*, *missio*, and *munus* in description of the activities of lay persons. In using these terms the council recognized a distinction between the activities of the ordained and the nonordained, while at the same time recognizing the *active* role which the nonordained have in the overall mission of the church and in the service of the Body of Christ. Perhaps most important of all, the council retrieved the original meaning of *diakonia* as service and emphasized the necessity of the ordained to look to the image of Jesus Christ the servant as model for their own exercise of ministry. As a result, increasing attention has been given to the understanding of *diakonia*, or service, as it is found in the New Testament, and to the relation between the services or ministries of the ordained and nonordained.

Ministry in the New Testament

What emerges from a reading of the New Testament, with an eye to the question of ministry as service, is that the gifts of the members of the Christian community differ. The ministries derive from the charisms or gifts of service, which are given by the Spirit in baptism. The action of coordinating these gifts, which has come to be understood as the ministry of the ordained, is also the gift of the Spirit. Each ministry is understood in light of the ministry of Christ the servant (Luke 22:24–27). Power in the church derives from his power (Matt. 28:18–20). The well-being of the church and its mission necessitates leadership and order. The early community looked upon the Twelve—or sometimes to others, such as Paul—to provide this service.

If one is content to pass over the ministries of the nonordained, then it is sufficient to offer a theology of ministry which views the power and authority of bishops and priests as emerging from the mission entrusted to the Twelve by Jesus—a power and authority passed on successively from bishop to bishop by laying on of hands. But if one strives to come to a fuller understanding of ministry, one which takes cognizance of ministries ordained and nonordained, established and unestablished, then other factors which derive from a reading of the New Testament need to be taken into account.

PAUL'S IMAGE OF THE BODY

Paul likens the church to a human body (1 Cor. 12:12–31). This analogy expresses the church's relation to Christ and his Spirit and is an effective expression of its unity in plurality. The analogy communicates the corporate dimension of the life of the church, as well as the personal participation which each one enjoys by membership in this Body and by the service which each one provides for its well-being and its mission. The various gifts, all of which are given for the service of the Body and its mission, contribute to this corporate life and mission.

EMPOWERMENT BY THE SPIRIT

Ministry is above all else a gift of the Spirit. Through the gift of the Spirit which calls members of the Body to its service, one participates in the mission and power of God in Jesus Christ. Empowerment by the Spirit is necessary in the life of the church since it is the work of the Spirit which keeps alive the remembrance of the life, ministry, message, and mystery of Jesus Christ. But it is also the Spirit's role to provide for new and creative expressions of faith and life in accord with what each new age requires for its own vitality. The remembrance of what God has done in Jesus through the power of the Spirit brings to the fore the church's future orientation. Through the action of the Spirit the church is constantly called to hope and to the future when God will be all in all. To live by the empowerment of the Spirit in remembrance of Jesus Christ is to live by a source of fresh creativity which calls forth new, and sometimes unprecedented, ministries to meet the needs and urgent demands of the age.

THE TWELVE: ESCHATOLOGICAL IMAGE

A more comprehensive understanding of ministry does not focus only upon the ministry of the ordained. A more inclusive theology of ministry does not view the Twelve primarily in terms of the mission entrusted to them by Jesus while he was on earth, which is then thought to be passed on from generation to generation of bishops and priests. Rather, the image of the Twelve is looked upon as an eschatological image of the whole church and all its members who, at the end of time, will be gathered at the banquet table when God's reign will be all in all.[8]

The Pauline image of the Body, an understanding of empowerment by the Spirit, and a recovery of the Twelve as eschatological image foster a fuller understanding of ministry which is better supported by the New Testament itself than is a view which confines ministry to the ordained.[9]

Types of Ministries

The understanding of ministry supported by the New Testament holds for a great variety of ministries. Nonetheless it is useful to look at several ways in which they might be distinguished from one another and classified according to type.

The Second Vatican Council offered a division of ministries based on the understanding of Christ as priest, prophet, and king. The contribution of both lay persons and the ordained are seen as participation in one or other of these dimensions of Christ's own ministry.

Another way of distinguishing ministries is to relate them to the church's life of *service*, *witness*, and *communion*. Thus some ministries would be directed to meet the needs of the internal life of the community (service), others more directly related to the church's mission of spreading the gospel (witness), while still others would be to nourish and foster the relations between and among the various communities of faith (communion).

Perhaps the most helpful classification, and certainly the most descriptive, is rooted quite directly in the New Testament. This classification distinguishes the various ministries in terms of *word*, *sacrament*, and *care*. It is based upon the listing of ministries in the Pauline corpus, such as Romans 12:6–8, Ephesians 4:11–12, and 1 Corinthians 12:4–11; 27–31, and upon what is known in other ways from the life of the early church.

The ministries of word are those of apostle, prophet, and teacher, but other services such as discernment of spirits would fit under this heading.

Little is said of the ministry of sacrament or worship in the whole of the New Testament. Efforts to base the origin of present-day ordained or "sacramental ministry" in what the New Testament says about the Eucharist or baptism—for example, that Jesus ordained the Twelve at the Last Supper or in the commission to baptize found in Matthew 28—rest on very shaky ground. Equally uncertain are the attempts to root these ministries of sacrament or worship in what is said of presiding within community, for example, in Romans 12:8.

Most striking about this classification is the significance attributed to the ministries of care. These include care of the sick (James 5:13–16), care of widow and orphan (James 1:27), healing (1 Cor. 12:9–10), and serving at table (Acts 6:1–6). It often happens that the term *diakonia* is used to describe only these services and not the other ministries. The result, curiously enough, is that they are seen as less important than the ministries of word and sacrament. But the contributions to the life of the church which fit into this category are not to be judged any less important or necessary. Their exercise in the life of the church, as well as the exercise of ministries of word and sacrament, does not call for mere repetition of what was done in New Testament days, but demands renewed and creative expression to meet the demands of the contemporary church.

This means that not all ministries which are being called forth in the church today find clear precedent in the New Testament or in the history of the church. It also means that it will be difficult to place the newly emerging ministries in fixed and ready categories. To recall what was said above in this chapter about marriage and the need for the ministry of marriage counselor, it is not immediately clear that such a ministry finds New Testament precedent. Nor is it clear whether such a ministry would be a contribution to the ministry of word, sacrament, or care. Awareness that new ministries may not find clear New Testament precedent, and may be difficult to categorize, should not cause resistance to their cultivation and recognition. Rather, it should stir up a sense of marvel and wonder in the face of the working of the Spirit which brings about diversity and variety in unity.

Ordained Ministry

There is a distinction both in history and in church teaching between the ministry of the ordained and other ministries. Yet, frankly, it is not quite clear what makes the difference. The recent attention to the ministry of the whole church as the People of God, with increased focus upon lay ministry, has left many confused as to what constitutes the nature of the ordained ministry, or holy orders. If asked, many would simply respond: the priest's job is to say Mass and hear confession. This response is not adequate, and gives evidence of a lack of awareness of the complexity of issues involved.

The ordained ministries, as distinguished from lay ministries, are those which are undertaken through sacramental ordination. All ministries, ordained and nonordained, established and unestablished, share in the universal priesthood of the People of God. The ordained ministries are three: the ministry of deacon, of presbyter or priest, and of bishop.

The diaconate, following the mandate of Vatican II, has been restored to a ministry in its own right. It is no longer merely a preparatory stage on the path to ordination to the presbyterate, or a ceremonial function. Celibacy is not a requirement for admission to the order of diaconate.

Presbyters or priests form a collegial body under the leadership of the bishop. Bishop and priests together are responsible for the pastoral care and direction of the local church, by building up the life of the church internally and by bearing corporate witness to and in the world through their style of life and work of spreading the gospel.

The ordained ministries specify a mission already given in the sacraments of initiation. It can be said of every adult Christian that his or her call and ministry is determined in light of the gifts of the Spirit given in the sacraments of initiation. For some, these are given official recognition through the sacrament of orders.

It is now more readily recognized that an understanding of the ordained ministry derives from and is dependent upon an understanding of church, and not the other way around, as it was thought in an earlier day. That is to say, the ministry of the ordained is dependent upon and shaped by the life of the church. Ministry is *from* the community and *for* the community. Deacons, presbyters, and bishops are called from the community and for the community. Consequently, the authority of orders must be related to the common, shared responsibility and mission of the whole church, and is unintelligible outside this context.

In accord with the wisdom of the Second Vatican Council, a contemporary approach to the ordained ministry views its contribution primarily in terms of service to the People of God, based upon the model of Christ the servant. In order to express the relationship between ordained ministries and the rest of the community at whose service they are, some recent theologies speak of ordained ministries in terms of leadership and presidency at the eucharistic assembly, rather than in terms of power, authority, and jurisdiction.

The distinction and the uniqueness of the ministry of the ordained are clearer when the Eucharist is seen as the source and summit of Christian life and the heart of the church's mystery. Then the ordained minister, the one who presides at the Eucharist, may be seen as a focal point of the church's relationship to God. Ordained ministry and authority are, in light of this, related to the service of the Body of Christ, the church, in faith and in worship. The role of the ordained may thus be understood in terms of the recognition, encouraging, and ordering of all the ministries in the community. This is done in a preeminent way through the role of presiding at liturgy, wherein the various ministries of a particular community are related to or connected to the larger communion of churches. It also relates the variety of ministries to the praise of God, precisely through the eucharistic celebration, the central act of worship in the church.

This is to take up the characteristics of the life of the church—apostolicity, unity, and catholicity—and relate the ministry of the ordained to them. That is to say, in the role of liturgical presidency the ministry of the presbyter is to keep the community in living continuity, or connection, with the tradition which has come through the apostles. The presbyter gathers into one body the various members around the table of remembrance, thus giving expression to the note of the church's unity. Finally, in the role of liturgical presidency the presbyter gathers the local community in faith and communion with all the other churches throughout the world, thus giving expression to the community's identity as catholic or universal. It is on this basis, at once apostolic and sacramental, that an understanding of the contribution of the ordained as a distinct, not separate, ministry rests.

Whatever is said of ministry, ordained or lay, the first and final word is that it is the Spirit who gives the gifts for the building of the Body. No gift may be judged inferior or less necessary to the Body. Likewise, gifts of service are not to be lorded over others. Such constitutes defilement of the Body and sin against the Spirit.

Tensions and Transitions in Ministry

Since it is now more commonly recognized that a theology of ministry and order derives from a theology of the church, the renewed ecclesiology born of Vatican II has resulted in a renewed vision and exercise of ministry. Such change has given rise to great discomfort and confusion among many, clergy and laity alike. Because of the great decline in the number of the ordained, many suggest that the church is in a period of great crisis. The vocabulary of the vocation shortage is familiar to most; vocation here is understood exclusively in terms of the priesthood or vowed religious life. Understandable as these expressions of confusion and frustration may be, they are more often than not indicative of a desire to return to a style of church life and practice which once was but is no longer, and is not going to return.

The present situation of ministry may be read as crisis. But within a moment of crisis there is also opportunity. Such opportunities are apparent in the present and in future directions of ministry.

Because ministry was once confined to the ordained, there are and will be multiple problems concerning the relation of the ordained to common ministries. In a former day it was quite clear what the function of the ordained was: say Mass, hear confession, anoint the dying and dead. In addition to these, other sacramental functions were provided by the ordained, as well as many or most other significant services to the community. Now it is not at all certain that such services belong to the ministry of the ordained by virtue of their ordination. Hence a variety of ministries have emerged in the life of the church and are now exercised by the nonordained. This is especially true of the base Christian communities in South America, Central America, Asia, Africa, and parts of Western Europe, but it is also true for the churches in North America.[10] The ministries of evangelist, catechist, teacher, reader, psalmist, cantor, minister of the Eucharist are now exercised by lay persons. In our own country the ministries of social justice and peace are undertaken by lay persons. Theological studies are undertaken by ever-increasing numbers of lay persons, and many assume posts in universities and colleges. Others work in more pastoral settings, serving the local needs of the community. In both cases the work of the theologian is a ministry for the building of the Body of Christ.

It is not feasible to provide an exhaustive list of the various ministries now exercised by lay persons. It would be even more impossible to attempt to list those ministries which will be exercised by the nonordained in the future as the church responds to the needs of local communities by drawing upon the variety of ministries given by the Spirit through baptism.

Besides the multiple problems concerning the relation of ordained to common ministries—tensions which will increase rather than decrease as ministry continues to go through transition—another problematic area is that of the institutionalization of some lay ministries.[11] This means that there is an attempt by the hierarchy at some level to designate, as a matter of course, a particular function. Hence there are movements to set up formal appointment to the ministries of catechist, evangelist, marriage counselor, or even that of lay leader in communities which have no ordained pastor. The same could be said for recent attempts to approve or appoint those exercising the ministry of theologian which is, in and of itself, a noncanonical vocation and ministry.[12]

Such practices may be viewed as helpful or as hindrance. The intention is often to promote recognition of lay ministries and to invite a wider sharing by lay persons in such roles. However, the procedures whereby recognition, approval, or appointment is given seem restrictive at times. For example, in the case of the appointment of "extraordinary" ministers of the Eucharist, or the installation of lectors, it can very easily happen that what of its nature belongs to all by virtue of the sacraments of initiation is in practice confined to a very few. To give the Body and Blood of the Lord to others, or to proclaim the word in liturgy, are ministries which should be able to be carried out by any mature Christian.

Tendencies toward institutionalizing lay ministries cannot be avoided, but ultimately the period of the institutionalization of such ministries will be short lived.

As the church moves toward the third millennium, less attention needs to be given to what is improperly referred to as the "vocation crisis." The present is a moment of opportunity for reading and responding to the signs of the times, illuminated by grace and Spirit. The task is not to lament the passing of a style of ministry and church life which is now gone, but to look in confidence and hope to the new vision of church life and practice which is emerging on the contemporary scene, especially in the basic Christian communities throughout the world.[13] This will require that the churches continually reshape their own self-understanding as the People of God and allow for the expression of forms of ministry in keeping with the meaning and message of Jesus and the gospel, but which may find no clear precedent in the New Testament or in church history.

Ethical Implications of Marriage, Ministry, Orders

In the sacramentality of marriage, the entire Christian community as well as the man and woman united live out of a vision of God's *personal, loving fidelity*. Christian marriage is thus the model par excellence of love and fidelity and provides a new way of living from the perspective of God's *self-sacrificing love* and *faithfulness* to the *divine promise*. The relationship between the man and woman together with their relationships with others are thus undertaken in light of the value of God's fidelity to the person and to the human community. The couple does thereby become a sign of God's own loving fidelity through their union with one another, and in their dealings with others in the human and Christian communities. Particularly through the bearing and rearing of children, fruit of faithful union and invitation to a more inclusive fidelity, the couple gives expression to the values of *self-sacrificing love* and *fidelity to promise*, and to the whole church's intention to live by these values.

In ministry is expressed the value of *service* to the human and Christian communities modeled on Christ's own service. It is rooted in the church's care of the various needs of the community throughout the ages and in remembrance of Christ's own life and ministry. Whatever advantages or disadvantages one may care to advance, the discipline of clerical continence and celibacy has been and remains an invitation to, and expression of, the faithful service of the community. All ministry—ordained and lay, undertaken by persons married or single—aims at giving concrete expression to the value of self-sacrificing love motivated by a new vision of reality shaped by the perspective of Christ's own *servanthood* and *faithfulness to God's promise unto death.*

Notes

1. For a brief but fine treatment of Christian marriage as a way of being and building the Body of Christ, see Monika Hellwig, *The Meaning of the Sacraments* (Dayton, OH: Pflaum Press, 1972), p. 69ff. See also Walter Kasper, *Theology of Christian Marriage* (New York: Crossroad Publishing Co., 1980).

2. See Bernard Cooke, *Sacraments and Sacramentality* (Mystic, CT: Twenty-Third Publications, 1983), chap. 7, "Christian Marriage: Basic Sacrament."

3. See Elisabeth Moltmann-Wendel, *The Women Around Jesus* (New York: Crossroad Publishing Co., 1982).

4. See Edward Schillebeeckx, *Marriage: Human Reality and Saving Mystery* (New York: Sheed & Ward, 1965). Schillebeeckx treats the reality of marriage as sacramental in and of its own nature vis-à-vis the Christian ritualization of it as such.

5. This account of the creation of man and woman is often selectively overlooked in favor of the account given in Gen. 2:18–25.

6. Bearing and rearing, or procreation and education of children, has often been viewed as the primary good of marriage within the Roman Catholic tradition. Some contemporary approaches to marriage and sexuality recognize two goods of marriage, the procreation and education of children together with the good of mutual companionship and love between the spouses, without placing one as superior to the other. Lisa Sowle Cahill speaks of these as commitment and procreative responsibility. See her *Between the Sexes* (Philadelphia: Fortress Press, 1985), p. 11.

7. See Yves Congar, *Lay People in the Church*, rev. ed. (Westminster, MD: Christian Classics, 1985).

8. See David N. Power, *Gifts That Differ: Lay Ministries Established and Unestablished*, 2nd ed. (New York: Pueblo Publishing Co., 1985), p. 101ff.

9. Ibid., chap. 4, "Learning from the New Testament."

10. See, for example, Michel Bavarel, *New Communities, New Ministries* (Maryknoll, NY: Orbis, 1983).

11. Power, *Gifts That Differ*, p. 154ff.

12. This is apparent in the new *Code of Canon Law* (1983), no. 812, which attempts to regulate and institutionalize the work of the theologian.

13. See the work of Bavarel, *New Communities, New Ministries*. See also Leonardo Boff, *Church: Charism and Power* (New York: Crossroad Publishing Co., 1985), p. 125ff.

8

Moral Decision-Making

In this chapter, a crucial point in our course of study, we will attend to the underlying principle of our approach to sacraments and morality, namely, that the sacraments themselves express a Christian morality. Then we will focus on the importance of conscience in its struggle to make choices informed by the ethic expressed in sacramental life. With the assistance of various models which provide methods for making decisions when faced with particular circumstances and choices, the ethical vision communicated in sacramental celebration is expressed concretely.

Morality: In Sacrament and in Word

The Spirit's presence sacramentalized in liturgy is the same Spirit which is to be sacramentalized in the actions and gestures which shape the Christian moral life. The Spirit *seized* and celebrated in liturgy and worship is the same Spirit *manifest* in the decisions, judgments, choices, and actions which together shape Christian living. The enactment of the life of the Spirit in liturgy and in daily life is sacramental activity. In short, we might say that the life of prayer and liturgy (contemplation) is surrender to the Spirit, while Christian moral life (action) is manifestation of the Spirit.

Christian worship and Christian living are like two sides of a coin. Christian living and the principles which guide the practice of the faith are rooted in the divine presence worshiped through word and sacrament. The Lordship of Jesus Christ and the power of the Holy Spirit are the keynotes of a Christian morality. The Lordship of Jesus Christ, particularly as we know this through the preaching, hearing, and appropriation of the word, provides the criteria to which the Christian submits all actions, decisions, and judgments. Here we might speak of the word of the Lord as providing the "objective criteria" for Christian moral life. It thereby recognizes no power, no judgment, no authority as absolute other than this Lordship. Everything is to be viewed in its light.

The power of the Spirit as a keynote of Christian morality expresses the importance of interiorization in Christian life, of acting in accord with the gifts of the Spirit, in the judgments, choices, and actions which are undertaken. This is a way of recognizing the need for taking into account the "subjective criteria" in moral living. The keynote of the power of the Spirit expresses the dimension of pneumatic guidance and the importance of the community of believers in one's attempt to live a Christian life. As a result, there is a need for discernment and for acting in accord with the Spirit, not the flesh (Rom. 8).

Sacraments: Expressive of Morality

Other approaches to Christian morality look to the normativity of Scripture or to natural law theory or to official church teaching as the focus for discerning the shape of Christian morality. Our approach, and the central thesis of this work, has been to look to the sacramental life of the church, to the church's worship in word and sacrament, as the focus for discerning the ethical horizon within which Christians are called to live, choose, and act.

In the sacraments of initiation, one is invited to a covenant morality, shaped by commitment and responsibility, which results from membership in the community of God's people. Hence morality is understood in terms of personal and communal responsibility and commitment to covenant, rather than blind obedience to moral norms. Christian moral life involves giving form to the original gift of grace and Spirit in baptism in the way we live and act. From this perspective, Christian morality is essentially a baptismal morality shaped, as are the baptized, by the Lordship of Jesus Christ and the empowerment of the Spirit.

The community of the baptized expresses and receives its identity as Body of Christ in the Eucharist. It is also in the Eucharist that a Christian ethic is most clearly expressed, and the ethical implications of sacramental life most evident. For the Eucharist expresses the Christian community's call and commitment to communion and justice. In this celebration are found the seeds of the whole meaning and message of Jesus.

Through the sacrament of penance the church expresses its continuing need for forgiveness, which results from failure to live out of the original gift of grace and Spirit given in baptism. In such expression the Christian community gives form to the new vision of reality by which it lives: from the perspective of God's mercy and forgiveness. Judgment of one's own life and that of others is made in light of the consciousness of sin and grace in the events of human life. Actions and decisions are undertaken in light of the fundamental perception of God's offer of reconciliation and forgiveness in the life and ministry of Jesus.

The sacrament of anointing is rooted in the church's care of the sick and in its struggle against illness, suffering, and depersonalization. Suffering and death are understood in light of the remembrance of Christ's own life and healing ministry, and in memory of his passion, death, and Resurrection.

The sacrament of marriage expresses the value of fidelity to promise and of self-sacrificing love. Marriage modeled on the union between Christ and church expresses a new vision of reality from the perspective of God's love and faithfulness. In its commitment to the integrity of marriage, and to the importance of children and family, the church gives meaningful expression to the values of faithfulness and love. Such values are not restricted to the life of marriage and family. Self-sacrificing love and fidelity in human relationships are required, not merely desired, of all who participate in the community of God's people by grace and Spirit.

The variety of ministries in the church, ordained and lay, give corporate and meaningful expression to the values of service and fidelity which derive from the model of Christ the servant. Through the variety of ministries, all of which are undertaken for the building of the Body in which God is glorified, the church holds up the value of self-sacrifice, service, and fidelity in the face of cultural currents and societal values which hold out a radically different vision of reality.

Word: Formative and Foundational in Christian Morality

In what has been said of the morality which is expressed in the sacraments themselves, it must not be overlooked that the proclamation and hearing of the word constitute an essential part of sacramental celebration.[1] Christian liturgy is worship of God through participation in the mysteries of Christ's love and presence in word and sacrament. Just as the sacraments are expressive of Christian morality, so this morality is founded in and formed by the word. That which is expressed in sacrament is proclaimed and heard in the word. Hence a well developed Christian morality looks not simply at what is expressed in sacrament but attends to the word, with particular focus upon the narrative of Jesus' life, ministry, and mystery and to the commemoration of what God has done in him, for the fullness of the ethical implications at the heart of Christian worship.

The covenant morality into which one is invited in the sacraments of initiation is illustrated more clearly in the proclamation of the word by which the Christian community learns of the moral responsibility of those invited to a new way of life brought about through a share in Christ's dying and rising (Rom. 6).

The call and commitment to communion and justice celebrated in Eucharist are more clearly expressed as the Spirit illumines the mind through the proclamation and hearing of the word. Through the effective proclamation of the word, the community hears the various stories which depict Jesus with food and drink. Consequently, Christians are better able to recognize the ethical implications of celebrating the Eucharist.

The sacraments of penance and anointing more clearly communicate the reconciliation and healing of God when seen in light of the Gospel stories that tell of the central role which forgiveness and healing played in the life and ministry of Jesus. The proclamation of the word enables the community to remember his ministry to the sick, suffering, and sinners, his call to repentance, his promise of forgiveness, and the acts and words by which he healed in God's name. Thus, through such proclamation, an ethical challenge is posed to the community which gathers to remember the one who was close to sinners and the sick and distant from the self-righteous and the powerful.

The ethical implications of ministry and marriage are all the more compelling when these sacraments are celebrated in contexts where Jesus is proclaimed in word as the servant of all, and in contexts where the promise of God's love and fidelity is announced time and again, thereby calling forth and enabling fidelity, commitment, and self-sacrificing love of God and one another.

Proclamation and hearing of the word in the liturgical assembly requires sound interpretation and explanation. Thus the crucial place of teaching and preaching in the life of the church cannot be emphasized strongly enough. Together with this, sustained and consistent reading and study of the Gospels and the entire Bible, by individuals and communities, contribute to an appreciation of the ethical implications of Christian faith celebrated in word and sacrament.

Keynotes of a Christian Morality:
The Lordship of Christ and the Power of the Spirit

Christian morality entails living out what is believed and expressed in worship. The Christian moral life is lived fully by engagement with the movement of the Spirit given in baptism through which we become children of God. To live by the Spirit, to live a moral life, is to be what we are, and what we know ourselves empowered to be. To live according to the Spirit, not according to the flesh (Rom. 8)—actions are to be understood as virtuous or vicious, good or evil, primarily in this light.

Perspective, not Prescription

In speaking of the morality expressed in word and sacrament a great difficulty emerges, for it is not always clear which actions are right and which are wrong, which are virtuous and which vicious. Problems arise which find no ready solution, and it is unclear which option or course of action is to be chosen.

To speak of a morality which is expressed in word and sacrament is to recognize that what is communicated is a vision, a horizon, a moral framework or sensibility. The sacramental life of the church expresses and impresses a general vision which has recognizable contours, and these we have seen. But this is a vision and perspective, not a bundle of moral prescriptions. The proclamation, reading, study, and hearing of the word enrich and expand the perspective which discerns in the sacraments a Christian morality. It is not to suggest that the Gospels or the Bible contain clear and precise moral prescriptions for each and every choice or course of action with which we are faced.

Christian morality is not simply a matter of appropriating preordained moral norms.[2] It is rather an active engagement with the movement of the Spirit of God which enables us to think, judge, decide, and act in accord with the criteria of the Lordship of Christ. Hence attempts to rigidly codify Christian morality usually result in legalism.

Christian responsibility is not complete in blind adherence to norms. Ideally, guidelines or norms should be followed as a manifestation of the Spirit discerned in one's own life, which leads one to recognize the true and the good which, to some measure, are expressed and safeguarded in norm and rule. Problems emerge, of course, when the true and the good, discerned in one's own life through adherence to the Lordship of Christ and the power of the Spirit, seem to conflict with rules and norms, even religious ones. Covenant entails the element of love, initiative, response, commitment, and fidelity on the part of persons and communities, made possible because of God's prior initiative and promise of fidelity. Though all of these elements are operative in a covenant morality, for the purposes of this treatment let us single out one: the role of responsibility in Christian moral life and decision-making.

The Role of Responsibility in Christian Moral Life

Through grace and Spirit given through the sacraments of initiation the Christian is enabled to make judgments and to live and act responsibly. Choice and responsibility are essential ingredients to mature life.[3] But it often occurs that in the life of Christian faith, adults do not really mature to the point of accepting responsibility for their decisions and actions. Such persons would recognize the importance of emotional, physical, and psychological growth, change, and development. They would agree that growth and change are necessary to relate to self and others in a responsible manner. Yet often such persons do not see the necessity of accepting responsibility for judgments, choices, and actions in the domain of Christian moral life, preferring instead an undue reliance upon the authority of priests and a naive understanding of the role of official church teaching.

Both society and church teaching provide us with norms and guidelines which enable us to think, judge, and decide how to act and be. They do not decide for us. The teaching authority of the church offers guidelines and principles which are intended to enable persons and communities to live out of the baptismal morality discerned in sacramental celebration and in word. The teaching of the church deserves careful attention and is to be given appropriate consideration in matters of faith and moral life. Such teachings are to be heard, and attempts made to truly understand what it meant by a given teaching. Church teachings are not to be obeyed unreflectively, blindly or out of ignorance. Nor are they to be obeyed because of childish refusal to decide or act responsibly.

The teaching office of the church, or the local parish pastor or confessor, is not charged with the responsibility to judge and decide for the Christian what Christian life is or what the Christian is empowered to be by grace and the Spirit. Church leaders and teachers are to guide persons and communities as they discern the movements of the Spirit and struggle to embody the original gift of grace and Spirit in the way they live and act. They instruct, and at times admonish, as Christians attempt to come to full personal realization of the ethical implications of what is celebrated in word and sacrament. Ultimately no one can judge, decide, and act for another. To deny or avoid the responsibility to judge and act is, in the final analysis, to refuse and deny the gift of the Spirit given in baptism by which we are empowered to do the truth in love freely.

Conscience in the Christian Moral Life

When all is said and done, one's conscience, above all else, must be obeyed in decision and action. In affirming the importance of conscience, it must be understood that conscience does not refer to a little voice that whispers in one's ear. Nor does it describe an inner feeling, pure and simple. Conscience needs to be developed and, above all else, informed, if one is to seek recourse to it in Christian life and practice. Further, conscience is formed in relation to others, and in communion with them, be it family, community, or church.

The term *conscience* has a twofold meaning.[4] First, conscience may refer to the habit or capacity, the basic sense of responsibility that characterizes the human person. Second, it may also describe the act of conscience, the judgment by which we evaluate a given action. Hence conscience describes a capacity in us and the activity of that capacity. Conscience in both senses needs to be developed through exercise. The capacity to choose and act must be strengthened by the very activity of judgment and decision itself. Through the gift of grace and illumination by the Spirit given in baptism, we are empowered to make judgments, to decide, and to act. Moral authority serves the function of guiding and informing, so that conscience, as both capacity and action, might be informed in light of the Lordship of Jesus Christ and the responsibilities incumbent upon the People of God. Conscience must be exercised, enlightened, and informed by the indispensable moral guidance of both church and society. That having been said, the judgments of conscience cannot be denied or its directives avoided by naive appeal to blind obedience to church teaching, the authority of the ordained, or allegiance to state or civil leader.

Neither word nor sacrament contains clear moral norms or prescriptions for ethical behavior. In the living out of what is professed in faith and worship, and in the realization of the original gift of grace and Spirit given in baptism, increased attention must be given to the dynamics of *understanding, judgment, decision*, and *action* as these are illumined by the power of the Spirit in light of the Lordship of Jesus Christ. Good choices are the result of the capacity and exercise of responsible judgments, informed by norms of church and society, and attentive to the movement of the indwelling Spirit who leads us to do the truth in love freely. But to speak of doing the truth in love freely is not the same as saying that an appeal to conscience justifies whatever it is that one chooses to do. Conscience needs to be formed, informed, and reformed through a process of ongoing conversion in Christ. This occurs through the action of grace in us by the indwelling of the Spirit, and by the action of the Spirit in others in community.

Models of Decision-Making

The morality expressed in word and sacrament is the horizon in sight of which concrete choices are made. In making such choices, models of decision-making are often quite useful.[5] They are like practical tools which enable us to accomplish a task. In this case, the task is decision or choice.

Models of decision-making are means, not ends in themselves. Like methods of prayer, their purpose is to enable the person to accomplish a higher aim, and hence to move beyond them. In employing various methods of prayer, the aim is to live out the desire for God, not to adhere to the method for its own sake.[6] The purpose of the models of decision-making described below is to enable persons and communities to make concrete choices, given the very practical circumstances which they face.

Models are basic patterns or mental structures which are devised to help in understanding and explaining how things happen.[7] In describing the five models below, the aim is to illustrate some of the ways in which Christians make concrete choices. The aim is also to enable the reader to become aware of the way in which her or his choices are made, and perhaps to adopt what may be useful from any or all of these models. No one model is sufficient to the degree that it could not be complemented by the advantages of another model. Further, the five models provided do not exhaust the possibilities. The reader would do well to consider what other model(s) might be useful in arriving at moral judgments or in decision-making.

The Normativity of Authority

One may choose primarily on the basis of the dictates of authority or authoritative norms.[8] Church teachings and official leaders are looked upon as ultimate bearers of authority whose words and judgments regarding Christian life and practice of faith are viewed as absolute. There is very little room for questioning or doubt. The problem is, however, that when it comes to the complex issues which face us in our own day, there are no easy answers.

The disadvantages of such an approach have been hinted at already in what has been said of personal responsibility and conscience. The real problem with this model is that the dynamics of interiorization, of attention to the movement of the Spirit who illumines the Christian to do the truth in love freely, are not given enough attention. Often the person simply responds to external codes and norms unreflectively, without attention to one's own capacity for understanding, judgment, choice, and action through the power of the Spirit dwelling within. Blind obedience is not to be extolled.

Pastors and confessors speak regularly of the difficulties which they face when people come asking them what they should do in a given situation. The tendency in us to want others to choose for us can be quite strong. In one sense it is much easier and indeed may seem safer to follow blindly. But the problem is that we often forfeit the great treasure of freedom, responsibility, and maturity which are ours through grace and Spirit. Many Roman Catholics express a growing sense of frustration when faced with the varied and sometimes conflicting directives of pastors and confessors in a given pastoral situation. That is to say, they get angry when they hear one priest say, for example, that those Catholics in second marriages are "living in sin," while another priest would recognize that, given varying circumstances, "living in sin" is not always the way such second marriages should be described. To many, this is a mixed signal from "the church" which they think "speaks" whenever the priest speaks. This reflects the basic difficulty which is posed when mature and responsible adults give inordinate attention to the directives of persons in authority, and avoid the responsibility for developing the capacity to understand, judge, decide, and act in accord with the Spirit.

The Normativity of Scripture

A second model of moral decision-making looks to the Bible for directives in making concrete choices. The person attempting to make a choice about a specific course of action would look for similar circumstances or dilemmas recorded in Scripture. One's choice would then be determined by the biblical account. For example, regarding a choice to marry or remain single, one might read what is written in 1 Corinthians 7 as the basis and determining factor for one's choice. Herein Paul indicates a preference for celibacy over marriage. Or one might look to Ephesians 5:21ff for making decisions about the way in which husband and wife relate to one another. The difficulty with this approach is that it lacks historical sensibility. The changes that come with history, for better or worse, are not taken seriously. There is often a rather naive application of principles which may have been appropriate to a former age but, in light of changed circumstances and a different historical context, need to be reinterpreted. So, for example, the historical situation within which Paul exhorted his readers to remain celibate is a much different one from our own. Paul was convinced that the end-time was near. Given the anticipation of the end, Paul concluded that it would be preferable to remain single. In our own day, perhaps we have lost sight of the significance of the end-times, and the potential destruction of the world signaled in the possibility of nuclear annihilation. But a deepened and renewed sense of the significance of the end-times which would emerge out of our own time and experience would not necessarily imply a reawakened sense of the priority which celibacy had in the mind of Paul. An overly facile reliance upon the literal word of Paul may be indicative of an unwillingness to recognize that it is the Spirit's movement within, together with attention to the word, which illumines the mind and stirs up the heart in love and truth.

The value of this approach is that it keeps attention fixed upon God's word in Scripture. In the life of certain persons, present and past, the literal reading of the Bible as a basis for decision-making has much to commend it. In the case of Francis of Assisi, who seems to have approached decision-making in this way, the literal reading of the Bible took place within the context of a deep immersion in the sacramental life of the church which was likewise understood to comprise and express a Christian morality. Hence Francis's literal reading of the Bible for concrete decision-making was deeply rooted in a sense of God's activity in history and presence to creation which is expressed in Christian sacramentality. Biblical literalism in the narrow sense overlooks the presence of God to creation and the activity of God in history. A literalist biblical approach disregards God's activity and presence in human life, world, history, and church. Its focus is exclusively on the revealed word in Scripture.

Following Christ

A third model of decision-making looks upon the life of Christ as a projected image of the self. One wishes to form and mold one's actions on Jesus, who is seen as the perfect model. The aim is to act in a Christ-like manner. The ultimate question is: What would Jesus do if he were faced with what I face? How would Christ behave in such a situation? How would Jesus approach the person with AIDS?

Would Jesus sit at table with this divorced and remarried person? How would Jesus deal with self-centeredness, self-absorption? How would he deal with maintenance men, kitchen help, cashiers, telephone operators? How would Jesus treat those seeking sanctuary in the U.S.? And so on. The aim is not to mimic actions of Jesus but to follow his conviction that God's Spirit guides, empowers, unifies, and heals.

This model has much to commend it. The model requires a familiarity with the way in which Jesus is depicted in Scripture. One is invited to cultivate a relationship with the Jesus revealed in Scripture. The relationship may take the form of master and servant, Lord and subject, friends, teacher and student, lovers, brother and sister, among others. Within the context of that relationship, one faces the moral judgments and concrete choices which are to be made. This model stresses the word and what is known of Jesus in other ways. It differs from biblical literalism in that it does not try to select principles from a text which would then be applied to one's own life. Rather, attention is given to the human self in relation with Christ. Because there is attention to personal relationship, there is room for cultivating and developing one's own experience, understanding, judgment, decision, and action. These are transformed by the person of Jesus remembered and rendered present through the power of the Spirit who enables Christians to have no other mind in them but the mind of Christ, and to act accordingly.

Interiority

A fourth model of decision-making looks more directly at the inner movement of the Spirit as the basis for moral judgments, choice, and action. Attention is turned to feelings, to inner sensibilities, as these are indicative of the Spirit's presence or the lack of the Spirit's presence. Many are familiar with this mode of decision-making as it is represented in the tradition of Ignatius Loyola.[9] Particularly helpful is what Ignatius has written about discernment of spirits.[10] Though he refined this approach to an extraordinary degree, the tradition of the process of discernment of spirits goes back to the early life of the church. John Cassian (d. 435?) provides criteria for the discernment of spirits in what he writes of the spiritual life.[11] Earlier still, we find in the writings of Paul a clear articulation of how one may know if one is acting in accord with the movement or prompting of the Spirit (Gal. 5:16–26). The aim of Paul, Cassian, and Loyola is to spell out criteria to guide choice and action in accord with what is perceived as the movement of the Spirit within. The

Spirit is understood to be manifest in those sensibilities or in those feelings which are in harmony with the fruits or harvest of the Spirit. For example, in considering option A, does the person feel a sense of peace or consternation? In looking to or imagining this option, let us say, for marriage, does she feel or sense herself joyful or troubled? In considering option B, let us say, going on for graduate studies, is there fear or confidence? Why? In deciding about volunteering a few years in Central America or the Catholic Worker House in New York's Lower East Side, is there restlessness or peace? Do I feel I'm going to volunteer to help others out? Do I sense that perhaps I may be the kind of person who *needs* to be needed? Am I going because I essentially feel guilty for the suffering in the world and, if the truth be known, would like to eliminate hunger and poverty by my own efforts? Is it perhaps the case that I want to go to Central America because I am basically hateful of my own family's upper-middle-class existence? Is hate a proper motive for doing anything? On the flip side, do I feel myself very comfortable with my family's upper-middle-class existence to the degree that my desire for that comfort prevents me from moving in directions that may require courage, perseverance, and a taste of long-suffering? These are the kinds of questions one would try to raise, and the kinds of feelings one would try to uncover in an attempt to work with this model of interiority for moral judgments and decision-making.

In brief and, it is to be hoped, without oversimplification, such a model aims at enabling one to make a choice which is in accord with what is felt or sensed as the presence of the fruits of the Spirit: peace, patience, joy, kindness, and the like. These are indications of how one might judge and act in accord with the Lordship of Christ and the power of the Spirit.

The value of this model is that it helps the Christian be more conscious of God's life within and the ways in which the Spirit moves. The problem of externalization or of unduly emphasizing "objective" criteria such as official authoritative teaching or the Bible, which characterize the first and second models, is not a temptation here.

The potential problem, however, is that of overinteriorization or subjectivism, resulting in a lack of attention to *the concrete facts of one's own life and history*. Because of an undue focus on the inner life it may be overlooked that God is active in human life, history, world, and church, and so attention must be given to various factors, not just the inner promptings of the Spirit. The word in Scripture also may be passed over. Hence the need for guidance, by someone familiar with the life of the Spirit and the ways in which the Spirit has been and is active in the Christian tradition, is particularly great when using this model of decision-making.

Values

A fifth model gives priority to one's values when making a moral judgment, a decision, or choosing a course of action. One would also need to sift through those values which one does not hold or consider very important. Choice then becomes a process of clarifying values and of bringing such clarification to bear upon one's choice. A typical question would be: Does this choice serve to realize and support the values which I hold? Does it, perhaps, conflict with those values, and foster countervalues; those values which go against the ones I hold dear and try to live by?

For example, someone is invited to the wedding of a former classmate. The wedding is to take place on the same date as a long-awaited weekend vacation. One may really want, indeed deeply desire, to go on the vacation. But upon articulation of the deepest values which one holds, which might include friendship, personal fidelity, and commitment, it may be clear that the better choice is to go to the wedding of the classmate. Or consider the scenario of trying to decide whether or not to attend a wedding of a relative who is being married "outside the faith," or in a nonreligious service. The person who holds friendship, personal fidelity, and commitment as high values may be led to a different decision than the person who places high value on the importance of religious observance and religious discipline.

The advantage of this model is that, through the articulation of values and countervalues, it enables one to get a comprehensive view of a given situation. Positive and negative factors are brought to light. Decisions are made on the basis of recognized meanings and values, and not simply on the basis of feeling or inner senses, or by appeal to some "objective" source such as the Bible or official church teaching.

The disadvantage of this model is that one may remain uncritical of the values upon which one makes a choice. Often we hear people say: "Well that's the way I am, like it or lump it." In like manner, some may be inclined to say: "This is what I value. This is what I think is important," without any real openness to question whether or not said values are valuable at all. For example, intimacy may be valuable. But the type of intimacy which is envisioned as excluding healthy and wholesome relationships with others needs to be critiqued. Generosity and availability are valuable. But if my idea of availability is one which allows me to be taken for granted, used, and violated, then my value of availability needs to be reevaluated. Hence the need for a critical eye and a willingness to reevaluate what one perceives and holds as meaningful.

Persons and groups who hold the values of hard work, the necessity of individual initiative and personal industry might be led to a very different decision when faced with choices having to do with U.S. economic affairs, than those who hold in high value the rights of the poor to the necessities of life. Persons who value health together with the dignity and sacredness of life have a better chance of making a mature and responsible Christian decision regarding issues of reproductive ethics than those whose only value seems to be the sacredness and dignity of human life— and this within a narrow focus. In any moral judgment or moral decision, there are values at stake. It is useful to be clear in spelling out the values which we hold, and to attempt to be consistent in the decisions we arrive at by appeal to these values.[12] If one espouses the value of the sacredness and dignity of human life, then abortion, capital punishment, and the nuclear arms race must all be seen as countervalues. Likewise, discrimination of persons on the basis of race, class, sex, or sexual orientation must be viewed as countervalues.

Concluding Remarks

Each of these models has strengths and weaknesses, advantages and disadvantages. Rather than looking at one model as that which provides the tool for sound moral decision-making, it is more useful to look to the various models and to what each may contribute to the process of making a mature and responsible decision. Each in its own way may lend something to the Christian community in the continuing quest to discover its identity as the Body of Christ in the world. In like manner, each model may lend something to the individual Christian in the daily struggle to recognize the traces of God's presence in his or her own life, and in the attempt to live by that original gift of grace and Spirit given in baptism.

The Importance of Consultation and Process in Moral Decision-Making

In the area of moral decision-making it is necessary to recognize the importance of the advice, counsel, and guidance of others in the church and in the larger human community.[13] Good choices are not made alone. They are made in dialogue with others, not only because the insight of wise and trusted persons throws light on our own struggle to make good choices but also because consultation brings to the fore the truth that our decisions and actions affect not only ourselves, but others in the human and Christian communities. The assistance of others in decision-making is required, not simply desired, if moral decision-making is viewed as one dimension in a much larger process of conversion of the whole person to the Lordship of Jesus Christ and the power of Spirit.

Just as the sacramental life of the church reflects the nature of conversion in Christ as a process, so moral decision-making is itself a process. Often we are inclined to look forward to *the* choice, *the* decision, *the* action which will settle all difficulties and tensions: the decision which will set us on our proper course. Sometimes we are inclined to look upon the choice of career or the choice for marriage in such a way. But as we have seen, the ultimate concern is conversion in Christ by adherence to the Lordship of Christ by the power of the Spirit. As a result, individual choices find their place within a much larger process in which conscience, as both capacity and exercise, continually develops. As conscience develops in the process of gradual conversion in Christ, judgment, decisions, and courses of action become more mature, more responsible. All choices are seen within the broader perspective of the draw of God's love through the Spirit and the Lordship of Jesus Christ. At times this will require that decisions previously made will need to be reevaluated and reconsidered in light of a more developed conscience, a clearer sense of the movement of the Spirit within, and a greater recognition of the Lordship of Jesus Christ.

Notes

1. See Bernard Cooke, *Ministry to Word and Sacraments* (Philadelphia: Fortress Press, 1976).

2. See Timothy O'Connell, *Principles for a Catholic Morality* (New York: Seabury Press, 1978). See also Richard Gula, *What Are They Saying About Moral Norms?* (New York: Paulist Press, 1982).

3. Bernard Häring, *Free and Faithful in Christ*, 3 vols. (New York: Crossroad Publishing Co., 1978–81), 1, situates the question of morality within the context of freedom and responsibility.

4. For a fuller treatment of this issue, see O'Connell, *Principles for a Catholic Morality*, chap. 8, "Conscience."

5. There exists a variety of models and methods of moral judgment and decision-making. J. Philip Wogaman provides a different, but useful, approach

to decision-making in *A Christian Method of Moral Judgment* (Philadelphia: Westminster Press, 1976).

6. Anthony de Mello makes this point quite well in his works on prayer. See his *Sadhana* (St. Louis: Institute of Jesuit Sources, 1978) and also his *Wellsprings* (Garden City, NY: Doubleday, 1985).

7. Bernard Cooke, *Sacraments and Sacramentality* (Mystic, CT: Twenty-Third Publications, 1983), p. 29ff.

8. For an approach which gives considerable attention to the role of authority in moral judgments and decision-making, see the work of Germain Grisez, *The Way of the Lord Jesus*, vol. 1: *Christian Moral Principles* (Chicago: Franciscan Herald Press, 1983), p. 831ff.

9. Ignatius Loyola's Spiritual Exercises provide key insights into the nature of discernment. See David Fleming, *The Spiritual Exercises of St. Ignatius: A Literal Translation and a Contemporary Reading* (St. Louis: Institute of Jesuit Sources, 1978).

10. There is a plethora of literature on this point. For a sampling, see John English, *Spiritual Freedom* (Guelph, Ontario: Loyola House, 1973), and also his *Choosing Life* (New York: Paulist Press, 1978).

11. John Cassian, *Conferences*, Conference 2, "On Discernment," translation and preface by Colm Luibheid, introduction by Owen Chadwick (New York: Paulist Press, 1985).

12. See "Cardinal Bernardin's Call for a Consistent Ethic of Life," *Origins* 13, no. 29 (29 December 1983): 491–94.

13. On this point there is a wealth of good literature. Spiritual guidance, spiritual direction, pastoral counseling are all distinct, but the concern in the final analysis is quite the same.

9

Sexual Ethics

An area of great delicacy in Christian morality is that of human sexuality. For many, Catholic morality and sexual ethics are virtually synonymous. That is to say, in the minds of many, Catholic morality has been and remains focused in a rather restricted way on the concerns of sexuality. However, even if Catholic morality has given extraordinary attention to the issues of sexual ethics and at times, at the level of practice, there has been a rather singular focus upon its concerns, it would be an inaccurate reading of the history of Catholic morality to suggest that it is concerned about little else. The issues of sexual ethics find their place within a much larger interest and concern for the whole person in community. Perhaps the narrow focus upon sexual ethics at various times in the history of the church stems from the overriding conviction that human sexuality is of fundamental importance in human beings' relationship with others and God. Because of its intrinsic dynamic toward intimacy with others and God, and because of its necessary role in personal love of others and God, sexuality from a Christian perspective has never been, and can never be, a question of "anything goes" or "whatever turns you on."

The Dignity of the Human Person

The human person is a sexual being. Concern about the whole person and her or his inherent dignity requires attention to the nature and function of human sexuality.

Cultural Obsession with Sexuality

In contemporary culture there is an inordinate focus upon human sexuality. Persons become viewed as sexual objects when the dimension of sexuality becomes focal in one's dealings with others, so that personal worth, capacity for relationship, desire for intimacy and fulfillment are overlooked. Everything is seen through the lens of sex. Look, for example, at the ways in which persons in contemporary society, even the very young, seem fascinated by those celebrities who thrive precisely through an appeal to sexual appetite. Personal worth and dignity are so often influenced by one's ability to perform sexually. Whole groups of persons define themselves primarily in terms of their sexual orientation. Others are labeled according to sexual behavior. The young are often not encouraged to advance toward sexual maturity, but forced through societal and peer pressure to engage in sexual activity long before they are capable of doing so in any other than a purely biological sense. The gravity of the situation is brought home to us by looking at the number of abortions among the young in our own country. Can a country with approximately one million abortions per year be said to be on the right track?

Catholic morality is not a Puritan ethic. Nor is it a single-issue ethic.[1] The concern with human sexuality at the heart of Catholic morality is focused upon the dignity and value of the human person and views sexuality from within that perspective. The aim of Catholic sexual ethics is to restore and maintain the integrity of human sexuality within an overall view of the human person.

Contributions from Human Science

A Catholic sexual ethic must be informed by principles of natural morality. That is to say, there is much that we can learn through advances in various sciences and disciplines which contribute more and more to an understanding of the nature and function of human sexuality. Empirical studies are able to help us more fully understand the collaboration between male and female physiology in reproduction. Through such advances, for example, the development of the microscope, it is now clear that woman is not a mere receptacle of man's seed; in any sexual activity between man and woman, she is an active agent, and not merely a passive recipient. On the contrary, medieval approaches to questions of sexual morality began with the assumption that the male seed contained within itself everything necessary for the conception of a human being, save the soil, or the receptacle for cultivation of the seed—the body of the woman.

Advances in knowledge also have brought to light the reality of constitutional, or irreversible homosexuality. The Christian tradition has been associated by and large with negative condemnations of homosexuality.[2] Empirical findings have shown us that homosexual orientation and relationship might be viewed differently than simply a person's willed perversion.[3] The phenomenon of homosexuality takes many forms, and it is far from being completely understood, but answers to the questions about the ethics of homosexuality must be sought in light of the growing consensus that most homosexual persons discover their sexual orientation as something "given," instead of something chosen.

Sexual ethics, then, must take such insights into any deliberation about the nature and function of sexuality. The needs and desires of the human person for pleasure and companionship, ecstasy and fulfillment, are all more clearly recognized when attention is given to the larger human enterprise, and in particular, those disciplines which help throw light upon the nature of the human person and the role of human sexuality.

Concerns for Human Rights

The various areas which advance the cause of human rights must also be given attention in any treatment of sexual ethics. It is not enough to speak of the image of God in the human person, and the value and dignity which derive from that affirmation, if one devalues woman as man's inferior and as the passive recipient and carrier of his offspring. Where the cause of woman is being advanced, and where hard-won rights are now beginning to bear their first fruits, Catholic morality must look for what can be learned in its own quest for a fuller appreciation of the dignity of the human person and a more appropriate articulation of the nature and function of human sexuality.

Needs of the Human Person

The human person has very basic needs. Catholic grade schoolers used to learn that the basic needs of the human person are food, water, shelter, and clothing. In many earlier approaches little attention was given to other dimensions of the human person aside from the physical, when speaking of needs.[4] But today, an adequate understanding of the human person would necessarily articulate the need, not just for shelter, but for proper and healthy environment. Such a contemporary approach also necessitates focus upon the need for *work*, in contradistinction to *labor*, the need for knowledge or education, and certainly the need for personal freedom.

Perhaps at a more fundamental level still, the human person has the need to love and be loved,[5] to be accepted and affirmed on the basis of who he or she is purely and simply, not because the person is wise or clever, but because he or she exists and, through acceptance and love, is capable of doing good. Such doing good is not itself the basis for love and affirmation. Rather, love and affirmation enable us to do good, and are themselves the condition for the possibility of our so doing. A clearer understanding of the need for love, and the need to love, may be gained by looking to the reality of human affectivity.

God's Love as the Root of Human Attraction

Christian faith affirms that by virtue of the person's existence as a created being, he or she is open to attraction by God and others. Not only is attraction to others and God part of what it means to be human, but the capacity for relationship and communion is based and built upon that very attraction. We are open, by virtue of being created, to the draw of God's love given concrete expression in the lives of other human beings. In response to that attraction there is at the same time response to God's love and attraction which makes all love and all attraction possible. Though it is often the case that there is little or no recognition of the draw of God's love at the root of all human attraction, Christian faith affirms this is the case. The God who is source and sustainer of all human life and love is the condition for the possibility of all deep attraction and real communion of love among human persons. Human attraction, inclusive of the sexual, is a noble thing, grounded in the mystery of the draw of God's love.

Affectivity does not describe a passing emotion or sentimental feeling.[6] Nor does it refer to fleeting passions or desires. Rather, affectivity describes that in us which is most basic and fundamental, the capacity to be touched by another from outside ourselves, and to touch another person.

Ecstasy, Intimacy, and Fecundity

To the notion of human affectivity must be linked an understanding of ecstasy, intimacy, and fecundity.[7] It is these which we desire, and for which we have the capacity, at the deepest level of our being. Such deep desires are linked to human sexuality, and fulfilled through the exercise of human sexuality whether in the union between man and woman, the choice for consecrated celibacy, or through other lifestyles and choices which are aimed at the mature and responsible integration of one's sexuality. In other words, that in us which is open to attraction by others and by God is the place which is touched in sexual love offered by another. Likewise, the deepest gift of self to another, the whole of one's person and one's deepest longing, is donated in love to another in the expression of that love in sexual union.

ECSTASY

Our desire for ecstasy is the desire to move beyond ourselves, to break out of our own skin, as it were, and transcend the confines of one's own limits. Ecstasy means to go out, to pass beyond. An ecstatic experience is one in which the subject breaks barriers, seems transported outside the confines of one's own limitations. It is one within which the person recognizes that he or she is not the center of the universe, that reality exceeds one's grasp, and that reality requires surrender and abandonment for true participation in it. Ultimately ecstasy is passing through the layers of illusion and self-deception to the point of self-donation to the other in abandonment and loving surrender.

Such ecstasy is the heart of the exercise of sexuality. It is through sexual expression that one gives of self to another, indeed one gives oneself over to another. Sexual expression enables one to cross over the limits of self in the donation of oneself to the beloved. Barriers are broken, paths are crossed, flesh is shared, self is offered and received, sources of life and personal centers are touched and brought into unity with each other. The two become one flesh. Yet sexual union, even of the most ecstatic sort, does not result in fusion of persons. The two are and remain distinct.

INTIMACY

In this breaking beyond oneself the need and capacity for intimacy is manifest. The human person is meant to live in communion with others. This communion is not simply a sharing of ideas or vision. It is rather a sharing at the deepest level of our being, inclusive of touch, tenderness, and pleasure. Intimacy refers to the desire to be held and to hold, to caress and be caressed, to bathe another in love and be bathed in love. Intimacy describes a union which is inclusive of sharing fears and tears, pain and suffering, thrill and excitement. It is that which each human person desires and for which each one longs. Sexuality is expressive of this need, and is a means whereby such a deep and abiding desire for communion with others may be met. But, as is obvious from contemporary trends in our own society, sexual expression is no guarantee of intimacy. Further, when sexuality is separated from its proper place within the more comprehensive scenario of the desire for deep and intimate communion of persons, the results are devastating. Put briefly, we are made for intimacy with God and others. Sexual expression lends to meeting the deep need for intimacy. Human beings were not created for sex, but sex was created for human beings and finds its proper exercise and expression within the context of the faithful, committed, intimate union of persons.

FECUNDITY

Fecundity describes the deepest potential within the human person for bringing forth life, the life-giving quality of human existence. At the most fundamental and natural level this is realized in the offspring of sexual union who are at once expression of sexual intimacy and ecstasy, and an invitation to a more inclusive love.

The opposite of fecundity is emptiness or barrenness, the inability or unwillingness to bear fruit, biological or other. Many people today experience themselves as empty or barren, even though they may be surrounded by children, blessed with health, have the chance to work, and enjoy a degree of prosperity and success. Here a useful distinction must be made between fecundity and productivity. Often those whose lives are empty are very productive, but are not fecund, or fruitful. In our attempts to be productive, we often try to ease our deepening anxiety about growing old and "useless." The products of our hands and of our minds often become idols. Not only are persons viewed and valued in terms of what they can produce, but persons themselves are often viewed and valued as products. When we view and value self and others in terms of productivity, we leave ourselves wide open for rejection, increased anxiety, and depression. Our real value rests in who we are, in the mystery and depth of the heart, not in what we can produce. Fruitfulness develops to the degree that we cease trying to produce by our own designs and devices. Both emptiness or barrenness and productivity are related to our attempts to control and manipulate the gift of life, and emerge from the inordinate desire for domination, security, and certainty. Fruitfulness on the other hand is cultivated as we gradually cease to control and as we begin to surrender to the rhythm and mystery of life—on its own terms. Fruitfulness is born of intimate and ecstatic love. Often this takes the form of children born of sexual union. Sometimes it does not. But if one surrenders in a relationship of intimacy and ecstasy, fruit results, biological or other. The fruits of a relationship built on love, and founded in love, are peace, patience, kindness, gentleness, single-hearted love, compassion, gratitude, and more. These are in no sense our achievements. They are gifts. They cannot be planned or predicted. There is always an element of surprise when they are given. When given, like all great gifts, we are humbled, numbed, and, at times, silenced by the generosity of the giver, and the greatness of the gift which is infinitely more than we could ask, deserve, or imagine. The fruits born of a relationship of intimacy and ecstasy have this quality of gift about them. As such, they stand in marked contrast to products, or the results of productivity, which are constructed by our own design

In this regard, it may be useful to broaden the context for our consideration of fruitfulness, because fruits of the sort spoken about here cannot be limited to the sphere of the interpersonal and the sexual. They are given within the context of interpersonal communion and communication with God, another, and others, it is true, but their effects move well beyond the personal and interpersonal so as to transform the social and political spheres, which are themselves disfigured and defaced by the work of our own hands. We need only consider the enormity of the tragedy we have inflicted on the human race and the ecological system in the name of productivity, efficiency, and technology. Millions die for want of nourishment, streams and rivers are polluted, natural resources have been squandered, and the earth and life are threatened by annihilation through nuclear war. This is what we have produced. But in what sense have our efforts been fruitful?

The fruits which are born of a relationship of intimacy and ecstacy—such as care, peace, gentleness, and compassion—have impact which far exceeds the couple in question or friends or family or community. Social and political machines are made up of persons and can be changed by them. The fruits of intimate and ecstatic union are to be passed on so as to be transformative of the world. The gifts received from fruitful union are to be passed on as gifts, enabling others to go forth and bear much fruit for the life of the world.

Marriage: Paradigm of Human Friendship and Sexual Expression

To speak of marriage as paradigm in the realm of sexual ethics is not to speak of marriage as norm, but rather as pattern or model. Not all persons are called to marriage. But in the Christian perspective sexuality and sexual expression should be evaluated by the criteria of faithful commitment and procreative responsibility, two abiding values which are regularly institutionalized in marriage.[8] These two values will not be realized by all persons given different relational, personal, and historical factors. Various persons will realize, achieve, or actualize these values of faithful commitment and procreative responsibility in greater or lesser degree, and in varying ways.[9] In attempts to formulate norms for guiding sexual behavior, norms which in the long tradition of the church have been viewed in terms of faithful commitment and procreative responsibility, more attention needs to be given to formulating criteria that define fidelity to the essence of this norm while allowing variance in the ways it is fulfilled.

In marriage the various elements of ecstasy, intimacy, and fecundity are expressed through sexual union and commitment to fidelity. The deep and abiding attraction of two persons for one another, and the affective needs of both are expressed through sexual exchange, inclusive of pleasure, tenderness, and excitement. Pleasure and excitement in the realm of the sexual are not extrinsic to the nature of Christian marriage, but are constitutive of it. In the fidelity and self-sacrificial love of man and woman, in their intimate sexual union, and in the fruit which is born of their union, be it offspring, the fruits of the Spirit, or both, marriage is the paradigm of human friendship and a disclosure of the fidelity of God.

Questions of Christian sexual ethics, then, must look to the elements of Christian marriage in making concrete choices. In the sacramentality of marriage, the Christian community, and the man and woman united, live out of a vision of God's personal and loving fidelity. Marriage is thus the paradigm of love and fidelity which provides a new way of living from the perspective of God's self-sacrificing love and faithfulness to the divine promise. The relationship between the man and woman, and their relationship with others, are thus undertaken in light of the value of God's fidelity to the person and to the human community. The couple thereby becomes a sign of God's own loving fidelity through their union with one another, and through their dealings with others in the human and Christian communities. Particularly, though not exclusively, through giving birth and rearing children, fruit of faithful union and invitation to a more inclusive love and fidelity, the couple gives expression to the values of self-sacrificial love and fidelity to promise.

All of the elements above may not come into play in making a concrete choice regarding this or that issue in the domain of sexual ethics. Nonetheless they do go together to shape a Christian ethic of sexuality. Decisions regarding sexual matters must, therefore, take account of the values of fidelity, self- sacrifice, the integrity of human persons, and commitment. Ethical decisions made purely on the basis of satisfaction, instinct, or the need for pleasure cannot be said to be good choices from the perspective of a Christian morality.

Again, it is helpful to recall the importance of the dignity of the human person, the dimension of human affectivity, and the needs for ecstasy, intimacy, and fecundity. Sexuality finds its place and proper expression within this context. Ecstasy may be understood, not simply in terms of sexual arousal and mutual or simultaneous climax, but as the total gift of the self which cannot be contained within the confines of one's own person, and which breaks those limits and overflows in self-donation to another.

Intimacy may be viewed as the bonding of persons in the deepest part of the self, given and received in sexual union. Tenderness, touch, caress, tears, and fear all go together to shape a notion of intimacy which flies in the face of the sentimentalized images of love and romance which are projected on screen, television, and in romance novels, and greeting cards. True intimacy is a strong and sober reality which includes tenderness and delicacy of touch. Again, sexual union does not guarantee, nor does it promise, the depth of intimacy for which the human person longs. Rather, sexual union presupposes intimacy of persons at the depths of personal being and is expressive of that union. It thereby strengthens it.

Fecundity likewise is not to be understood simply in terms of children born of the union. They are an expression of the sources of the life-giving potential of the couple. Such life-giving potential is manifest in the gifts of gentleness and care, thanksgiving and compassion which are offered to those with whom the couple comes into contact. These are gifts born of the union between two persons; they are not products. Gifts received are given freely by those who live a fruitful life. This may be made clearer by reflecting upon whether or not most couples view their union as a real source of life and nurture for those other than their own children. Do couples look to their bond of fidelity grounded in sexual union as a wellspring of life from which gifts flow for the life of the world?

All of these elements go together to shape a view of sexuality within the context of personal value and dignity. Sex is not an instrument; nor is it a part of the person which can be separated off from the rest. No matter how hard one might try, sexuality cannot be denied or dealt with as if it did not exist. The person is a sexual being and, consequently, matters of sexual ethics cannot be settled by simple appeal to abstract principles or unreflective allegiance to moral norms. Sex in itself is something of an abstraction. It is human beings who express themselves relationally and personally in particular historical contexts through sexual activity. Recent attempts to treat sexual morality are more willing to take the personal, relational, and historical factors into account than most earlier approaches. Sexuality is viewed not simply as an appetite, but as a vehicle of total self-expression. Thus one contemporary approach looks upon sexuality not simply from the perspective of the faithful union of spouses and their procreative responsibility, but in the much larger context of sexuality's role in persons' "creative growth toward integration."[10] From this approach, sexual activity is to be evaluated in light of seven values. It is to be self-liberating, other-enriching, honest, faithful, socially responsible, life-serving, and joyous.[11]

In the various concrete choices which persons face, those values which are expressed in Christian marriage must be looked to as they shape a Christian sexual ethic. Yet in the attempt to realize and incarnate those values of fidelity and self-sacrificial love, persons will be faced with the challenge of doing so in varying circumstances wherein unique and concrete factors need to be considered. Again, the need for models or methods of decision-making.

Criteria for Judgment and Choice in the Realm of Human Sexuality

In looking to Christian marriage as paradigm of human love and friendship, we have seen the morality which the sacramental life of the church itself expresses. Recalling what was said in chapter 8, this sacramental ethic provides principles which inform one's perception and perspective. Given this sacramental perspective, there is need for methods or models which may be likened to tools which help us to tackle the job of decision-making, to draw out the practical implications of that vision of Christian life expressed in word and worship.

This ethical vision expressed in the sacramental life of the church is not the single criterion for making choices in the area of sexuality, or in the evaluation of sexual activity. It has been pointed out earlier that the word, or the Bible, is likewise to be given considerable attention in the area of moral decision-making. To these must be added the long tradition of the church, and the currents of philosophy in the tradition which have attempted to establish essential convictions and norms regarding what sexual activity *should* or *must* be in light of a comprehensive vision of reality. And to all of these must be added the findings of contemporary empirical studies which attempt to describe how people actually behave sexually.[12] All of these provide criteria for making choices and judgments regarding human sexuality. No one of these criteria can stand alone. Each complements and corrects the other. For example, the biblical injunction to be fruitful and multiply (Gen. 1:28) would need to be nuanced in light of empirical studies regarding the health and well-being, both biological and psychological, of women during child-bearing years, as well as the problem of diminishing ecological resources. Or, on the other hand, the norms regarding what sexuality should, might, or must be, which have rather constantly guided the tradition of the church, offer a corrective to a contemporary view which regards abortion as just one more form of birth control.

Faced with a Choice

In light of our five models for moral decision-making it may be useful to recall the essential contours of a sexual ethic expressed in the sacrament of Christian marriage. Imagine a young woman faced with a choice. She has reached a certain point in her life which seems to require that she choose to marry, pursue a life of consecrated celibacy, poverty, and obedience, or remain single. All three choices are ways of integrating one's sexuality in terms of a life project. No one is objectively superior or better than others, though faulty understandings of sexuality, contemplation, and ministry have often resulted in claims that priesthood and religious life are better ways of life than marriage or the committed single life.

In marriage the life project involves one other person in an intimate relationship, and whatever children may be the fruit of the union. In the choice for consecrated religious life the project includes significant others with whom one is bonded in a community of service and witness in the church. In the choice for the single life the life project includes a large measure of personal freedom and self-determination together with deep friendships. These are viewed as necessary for the purpose of the life project itself. In some cases the life project of the single person may be the direct service of the church.

Faced with these three options, which are not as clear cut as once they might have been, the person is challenged to decide which is the best way to live out the desire for God, the fullness of grace and Spirit given in baptism, and in so doing find happiness and fulfillment with oneself and others.

We might depict the person faced with a choice using the various models of decision-making in the following way.

At first the person might attempt to listen within the self to the deep longing and movement of the Spirit—we hope, with the aid of an adviser. However, even with the aid of this director, there is no clarity. When she considers the option for marriage, she is filled with peace, contentment, well-being. In considering the option for consecrated religious life, many of the same feelings are present. Though her sense of well-being and peace in considering the committed single life is not as strong, neither are there strong negative feelings such as loneliness, anxiety, despair. The model of interiority treated earlier is not of much assistance to her, at least not apparently.

Next, she goes to the Scriptures themselves in an attempt to throw light on the various options from which she must choose. The Scriptures depict Jesus as one who held marriage in high regard, yet as far as we can determine was himself a single, celibate man. Paul writes of the value of remaining unmarried, but the circumstances which Christians faced in his day were quite different from our own. Further, about religious consecration, or "religious life" as we now know it, the Scriptures say little or nothing. Again, the person faced with a choice has seemingly gained little clarity and is unable to choose from among the options. The second model proposed earlier, the normativity of Scripture, has not been a useful tool, or so it seems.

Light is thrown on the situation only when she takes Christ as the projected image of herself, and raises the question: What would Jesus do if faced with these circumstances, if given this choice? When considering the option for married life, the person would have to recognize that in married life the issue is not so much one of imitating Jesus' acts but of following and living by his conviction that God's Spirit guides, empowers, unifies, and heals. Slowly and gradually clarity comes. She begins to see that way in which she is called to follow Christ. The life project and the best way of integrating her desire for God and her desire for others emerge after time, through the process of prayer and consultation. The third model treated earlier has been most helpful here. The other models may have thrown some light on the question, but it was the model of discipleship, or following Christ, which provided the tool which enabled her to make the concrete choice. The other models, the normativity of authority and choosing on the basis of value, might also have been used to throw light upon the situation.

Some may question the appropriateness of using such a case as an example of how matters of sexual ethics are decided. Such a question is likely to emerge if one has not yet grasped the place of sexuality within the much larger context of the dignity of the whole person. The various choices which we face all draw upon us as total persons, inclusive of the sexual. The choice for career or for lifestyle, for single or married life, entails selecting one way from among many, in light of the task of integrating one's sexuality in terms of a life project. Hence it may be understood as a concern in a treatment of sexual ethics.

Persons facing other choices in the area of sexual ethics must do so in light of the moral horizon expressed in word and worship and with the assistance of various models of decision-making. Again, this must be done with attention to the long tradition of the church, and the philosophical currents within that tradition which have attempted to spell out what sexual activity ought, should, or must be. But to these factors must be added insights from the empirical, social sciences which indicate or describe how people really are and act sexually. Judgments about homosexuality, in light of these various factors, might be arrived at by using the model of choosing on the basis of value together with the model of following Christ. How would one then respond to homosexuals if one chose to imitate Christ by following Christ's conviction that God's Spirit guides, empowers, unifies, and heals? How would one look upon homosexual relations and acts? What values are operative in one's life in dealing with homosexual persons? Compassion, friendship, reconciliation? Security, certainty, upholding what is perceived to be "the way it should be"?

Example after example could be offered. One would do well to consider the questions of responsible parenthood using the various criteria and models for decision-making. But rather than cite a list of examples, it might be useful for readers to "unbuckle" their imaginations to consider how each model might serve them in light of the moral horizon expressed in word and worship and in light of the other criteria which need to be taken into consideration in judging and choosing in the area of sexual ethics. Here again, it must be stressed that questions of sexual ethics should be evaluated in light of the suggested norms of faithful commitment and procreative responsibility. Particular expressions of sexuality will realize these norms to a greater or lesser degree and in varying ways. Ultimately the issue is one of being faithful to the essence of the norm while allowing variance in the way it is fulfilled.

Here it is useful to note that one may at a later time make a choice which requires the reevaluation of an earlier choice made in good conscience. Future choices require that previous choices be reappropriated, sometimes in new and different ways, in light of a more developed conscience and a deeper sense of personal responsibility and capacity for judgment. There is no one choice which, once made, eliminates the need for mature and responsible decision-making in the future.

No Easy Answers

This chapter cannot be expected to give answers to the many questions which face contemporary Christians. Its purpose is simply to draw attention to the morality expressed in the Christian sacramentality of marriage as paradigm of human love and friendship, and to point to the various models of decision-making as they might assist in choosing from among the various options which one must face in the realm of sexual morality. In any choice regarding human sexuality, attention must be given to fidelity, self-sacrificial love, human affectivity, ecstasy, intimacy, and fecundity. These elements must enter into any decision-making process concerned with a Christian morality—even more so when complex issues are involved.

As much as one might hope or insist otherwise, premarital sex is quite a common practice in our own day. Many who choose this option do so on the basis of a rather individualistic and privatized approach to sexual ethics. The frequent response to criticism of premarital sex is that two persons should be able to do with their own bodies what they wish. But it must be stressed that the values and principles at stake are not purely personal and/or individual ones, but are values held and shared by the community, religious or otherwise. Sexuality has social significance and is never simply a question of "bedroom" ethics. Choices are shaped by a communal ethos and affect that ethos in turn. That is to say, strange though it may seem, what two people do in bed does have implications for the larger human and Christian communities.

When considering the question of premarital sex in light of the moral horizon expressed in word and worship, one must realize that sexual intercourse is not only for the purpose of giving concrete and tangible expression to personal, intimate relationships and affective needs. It is also an expression of accountability and fidelity. The relational and affective as well as accountability and fidelity are all dimensions that are sacramentalized in sexual union. The question would then have to be raised as to whether a couple engaging in premarital sex recognizes the responsibilities and commitments which are implied in the act which is of its nature a concrete embodiment, or sacramentalization, of one's accountability and fidelity to the other.

Another complex issue is that of artificial birth control, or contraception. Some would suggest that contraception enables two persons to pursue certain values such as intimacy, deep and lasting friendship, mutuality, and stability. Others maintain that contraception thwarts one of the purposes or ends of Christian marriage, namely, the procreation and education of children. Ultimately the question is whether or not contraception can be integrated into a marriage which is truly Christian. Some decide that it can, because it enables a couple to pursue the values of fidelity, intimacy, and real sharing in personal communion. Others insist that it cannot because it thwarts one of the goods of marriage, and leads to a contraceptive mentality.[13] Such a contraceptive mentality, which looks to life as a product to be controlled and predicted rather than as a gift to be received, is a real danger and must be brought into any mature and responsible decision-making regarding contraception in individual cases. Responsible parenthood, which goes hand in hand with cooperation between the sexes in matters of reproductive ethics, is one of the most pressing issues facing the churches. But the complexities of the issues involved are well beyond the scope of this work.[14]

Sexuality has its place within a larger vision of the human person. Through it the Christian participates in the love of God and Christ. But such participation does not make decisions for us.

A Christian view of sexuality emphasizes the goodness of committed sexual relationship, and the singular significance of faithful commitment. Within this context, procreative responsibility is seen as central to the nature of sexual relationship. As a result, a Christian sexual ethic finds itself increasingly at odds with the morality of secular culture which seems to deny the necessity of integrating one's sexuality within an overall life project and within the framework of faithful commitment as a primary moral mandate. But the task of this integration, of becoming fully human, is lifelong. Faced with such realities as divorce and remarriage, responsible parenthood and homosexuality, the greatest need within the church in the area of sexual ethics is the formulation of criteria which would help people to recognize how they can be true to the essence of the twofold norm of faithful commitment and procreative responsibility given the varying personal, relational, and historical situations in which they find themselves. To this end, perhaps we need a deeper awareness of the grace that "slips between the cracks," inviting even those in "irregular" and "nonnormal" relations to be faithful to the essence of what is embodied in the norm of faithful commitment and procreative responsibility.

Notes

1. See "Cardinal Bernardin's Call for a Consistent Ethic of Life," *Origins* 13, no. 29 (29 December 1983): 491–94. See also Cardinal Bernardin's Report to the Bishops, "The Value of the Consistent-Ethic Approach," *Origins* 14, no. 24 (29 November 1984): 397–98.

2. See John Boswell, *Christianity, Social Tolerance, and Homosexuality* (Chicago: University of Chicago Press, 1980).

3. See Robin Scroggs, *The New Testament and Homosexuality* (Philadelphia: Fortress Press, 1983).

4. A real departure on this point was the encyclical letter of Paul VI, *Populorum Progressio*. The encyclical letter of John XXIII, *Mater et Magistra*, also attempts to resolve social questions in ways more in accord with satisfying deeper needs. See both in Joseph Gremillion, *The Gospel of Peace and Justice* (Maryknoll, NY: Orbis, 1976).

5. For a fuller treatment of these needs, see Jean Vanier, *Ton silence m'appelle* (Montreal: Éditions Bellarmin, 1980), p. 60ff.; or my treatment of these in *A Blessed Weakness: The Spirit of Jean Vanier and l'Arche* (San Francisco: Harper & Row, 1986), p. 61ff.

6. For a fuller treatment of the notion of affectivity, see Michael Downey, "A Costly Loss of Heart: The Scholastic Notion of *voluntas ut natura*," *Philosophy and Theology* 1, no. 3, (Spring 1987): 242–54.

7. This threefold framework is derived from a series of lengthy personal conversations with Jean Vanier during the summer of 1981. They are treated briefly in my doctoral dissertation, "An Investigation of the Concept of Person in the Spirituality of l'Arche as Developed in the Writings of Jean Vanier" (Washington, DC: Catholic University of America, 1982), p. 155ff. These same themes are taken up by Henri Nouwen, *Lifesigns: Intimacy, Fecundity, and Ecstasy in Christian Perspective* (Garden City, NY: Doubleday, 1986).

8. Lisa Sowle Cahill, *Between the Sexes* (Philadelphia: Fortress Press, 1985), p. 148ff.

9. Ibid.

10. Anthony Kosnik et al., *Human Sexuality* (New York: Paulist Press, 1977), p. 86.

11. Ibid., pp. 92–95.

12. Sowle Cahill, *Between the Sexes*, p. 10.

13. See, for example, the encyclical of Paul VI, *Humanae Vitae: Encyclical Letter on the Regulation of Birth* (Washington, DC: United States Catholic Conference, 1968).

14. For a useful exposé of the issues, see the work of Sowle Cahill, *Between the Sexes*.

10

Social Justice Ethics

Faced with the challenge of implementing the principles of the gospel in the socio-political order, some express great dissatisfaction for they divide religion and politics into two separate spheres, having little to do with one another.[1] Many decry the political activities of church figures as meddling in areas of life where they ought not to be. Still others do not mind the church lifting its political voice, as long as what is spoken of is their brand of politics. Others recognize that the church does have a mission in the political order, but would assign this mission exclusively to the laity. Hence, according to this position, clergy and religious have no business in politics. The other side of this position is that lay persons have no business in the decision-making and official life of the church.

In chapter 9 we saw that it is now more commonly recognized that a Roman Catholic approach to moral life does not focus upon one dimension of human life, for example, human sexuality. A Catholic ethic is, rather, concerned with the whole person, not just this or that dimension or area of human life.

To recognize this is to acknowledge at the same time that no human being exists alone, in isolation. From the very first moment of existence, the human person is in relationship with others. To be human requires the development of such relationships with others, as one moves into broader and broader spheres of interaction: from parents, to family, to extended family, neighborhood, school, community, and so on. This movement is illustrative of the social dimension of the human person. An ethic, then, which is concerned with the whole human person and her or his dignity must attend to human actions as they affect others in the larger social arena, and to how the larger social sphere influences and affects the individual. In brief, the relational, salvational, and political are all of a piece. They are different areas in which God is active and present.[2]

160

Contours of the Kingdom: In Word and Worship

In word and worship Christians proclaim Jesus as savior of the world, yet it is often the case that the world is looked upon as intrinsically corrupt—indeed beyond salvation in any real sense. In liturgical celebration we sing of Jesus as prince of peace, many of us meaning some sort of interior peace of heart or mind, because we simply have written off the possibility of world peace, or any meaningful change in the warlike actions of nations. Christ is lauded as king of the nations, yet deep within the Christian psyche is embedded the conviction that the kingdom is not of this world. Jesus is proclaimed to be Lord of history, but in reality "salvation history," so that the rest of the human story is understood to be outside God's concern, and our own. All that is to be said of it is by way of negative judgment.[3]

All of the above perceptions reflect a dualistic view of the Christ which results in a dualistic view of church and world, faith and politics, liturgy and life. Various dualisms which have afflicted Christian history have often been supported by official church teaching, though the spirit and letter of the Second Vatican Council have provided the possibility for overcoming such dualism, particularly as regards the relationship between church and world, religion and politics.[4] The single most difficult problem which results from a dualist perception of church and world is that God's grace and activity are relegated to the sphere of the sacred. God's presence is confined to the sanctuary, to holy persons, and to holy times. A sacral world view results, not a sacramental one.

This sacral, dualist world view issues in privatization of religious belief and practice, and fragmentation of the various dimensions of life into various parts. Hence we hear talk of one's "prayer life" or "spiritual life" in contradistinction to one's ordinary, daily, "worldly life." Recent efforts to engage in reflection upon the social implications of the Christian life have attempted to overcome this false dichotomy which relegates religious sensibilities to a very short span of time on Sunday, and perhaps to brief periods of prayer or worship during the week; which places the rest of one's relational life, inclusive of the social, sexual, and political, outside of the domain of the sacred.

To bridge this gap, a gap which is a false construction to begin with, many recent efforts have focused upon providing very particular moral prescriptions that address particular social and political issues. One is reminded of the social and political implications of one's Catholic commitment from pulpits as government elections approach. Often this takes the form of specific moral exhortation regarding the absolute necessity of voting for "pro-life" candidates. Rarely do ordinary Catholics receive such direct moral exhortation on other socio-political issues, and many resist this approach. The establishment of norms and prescriptions for particular courses of action in the face of particular concrete issues and choices does not seem to provide the key to overcoming privatization and fragmentation in religious belief. Nor does it seem to lead to a sense of corporate, social Catholic identity. For all protestations to the contrary, there does exist a plurality of opinions on the issue of abortion. That is not to say, however, that the various positions are equally acceptable or compatible with Catholic identity.

The split between church and world, the dualism which still colors our vision of faith and politics, and the privatization and fragmentation which characterize the way we approach liturgy and life will continue as long as the "sacral" view of the world, God, self, and others continues. To overcome this dualism, we will need to recover a truly "sacramental" world view.

The key to such a recovery is nestled within the long and rich tradition of Christianity. Because the Roman Catholic church is a sacramental church, our approach to God, world, self, and others is marked by the conviction that God is active in history and present to creation. Coupled with this is the increasing and ever-growing belief that God's grace and presence, which are available to *all* people by virtue of their creation, are particularly and uniquely present in the church, especially in its sacramental life. In its sacramental celebrations, the Christian community expresses its belief that God is active and present, not *on* human life, history, world, and church, but *in* human life, history, world, and church. What follows from this, then, is the conviction that each of the seven sacraments is a specific and particular manifestation of the universal offer of God's life and presence. The very enactment of the sacrament, then, points beyond the sanctuary and its enactment speaks not only to the personal, private dimensions of life but to the relational, salvational, and political dimensions of human life, world, history, and church.[5]

Human beings are not usually motivated by direct appeals to their wills, but by being touched in their imagination. *Imagination* refers to the affective, emotional, intellectual, and volitional center of the self,[6] not to mere fantasy or antinomian irrationalism. In terms more familiar to biblical writers, and to Christian spirituality, we are speaking of the "heart."

When the imagination is touched, when heart speaks to heart, then possibilities for responsible Christian action increase. Awareness of the social and political dimensions of Catholic Christian life will grow to the degree that we cultivate and appeal to the moral imagination, the thinking and responsible heart, of Christians.

This moral imagination is cultivated and shaped in a singular way in the church's worship. Perhaps no symbol or image is so compelling in its appeal to the Christian imagination, as that of the kingdom, or the reign of God. The reign expresses God's intention for the world both now and to come. It bespeaks right relations and the reversal of "the-way-things-are-because-that's-the-way-it's-always-been" mentality which limits creativity, alternative visions, and hope for the future. It is a word of mercy, compassion, peace, justice, forgiveness, and truth. And the Lord of this kingdom is a lord unlike any other, whose power and authority reside not in right, privilege, or ability to dominate and control, but in loving service unto death. If it is conceived of as a place, the kingdom might be envisioned as a banquet, where the poor and the wounded, the weak and the vulnerable are seated at the table of honor; Jesus himself having relinquished his place there.

It is in the word and worship, the sacramental life of the church, that the contours of God's kingdom, whose hallmarks are justice and peace, are most clearly discerned.

Social Sin

The privatization and fragmentation of religious living has colored our perception of not only God, self, and others, but of sin and sinfulness. In the past, sins against the seventh commandment dealt with injuries done to immediate neighbors, such as stealing or harming a neighbor's property. These are still recognized as sin, as indeed they should be. But a contemporary approach to morality would also look to racism, classism, sexism, sacralism, environmental pollution, militarism, and other such realities as sinful. Not simply a question of determining whether individual actions of a person are sinful, such a contemporary approach recognizes that sin and evil have become woven into the very structures of the social order and that such sin affects the lives of many persons, keeping them helpless victims, incapable of acting maturely and responsibly—as subjects of their own history.

Racism thrives on the basis of affirming the superiority of

one group of persons over another, solely and purely on the basis of skin color. Sexism is built upon the subordination of one sex to another, relegating women to positions of inferiority and submission solely on the basis of sex. Classism flourishes when whole groups of people are oppressed because of the social class or caste into which they are born. Environmental pollution destroys the harmony and ecological balance of the earth so that the few reap benefits while the many have little or no earth left. Sacralism thrives when the few who are relegated to the realm of "sacred duties" present obstacles to the many who strive to live out of the desire for God, thereby thwarting the possibility of persons becoming subjects of their own religious history. Militarism attempts to keep thousands, sometimes millions, in a state of forced tranquility through power, domination, arms, and the threat of violence.

In a former day, not much attention was given to the reality of social sin. Sin describes a willing participation in evil. Social sin describes not what we do directly, but what we are accomplices in doing. At root, social sin refers to the corporate nature of human sin. More particularly, it refers to sin as it is embedded in structures of government and political practices which keep persons and groups from living in accord with the value and dignity which is theirs as persons. Social sin is manifest in policies, practices, norms, and structures of the socio-political order which thwart the human person's call and challenge to do the truth in love freely. Such sin blocks the human person and makes it nearly impossible for her or him to become a subject of her or his own history. It keeps history, society, church, world, family, and community in someone else's hands. The reality of social sin thwarts human agency, dignity, and destiny through the enactment—at times willed and systematic, yet more often unconscious—of policies and structures which defy the dignity, value, and rights of persons and communities.

A social justice ethic is concerned with the response required of Christian persons and communities in the face of the reality of social sin. Since, ultimately, social sin robs the person of rights and dignity, social justice is concerned with assuring those rights and that dignity, and creating a world within which all may grow. To speak of social justice ethics necessarily demands, then, that attention be given to the socio-political ramifications of the gospel and to the socio-political ramifications of what is professed and expressed in Christian faith and worship in word and sacrament. A Catholic morality is not simply concerned with a relationship between "me and Jesus." A fresh reading of the gospel requires, not simply desires, attention to the reality of social sin and to those activities which will assure a world in which all may grow.

The Dignity and Rights of Person and Community

As was seen in chapter 9, a contemporary approach to Christian morality must look to the various disciplines and sciences of the human enterprise in the formulation of an ethic. That is to say, principles of natural morality offer valuable contributions to the continuing effort on the part of Christians to meet the demands of the social implications of the gospel.

Forming Coalition with Others

The Christian community must learn from those movements where the crusade for human rights and dignity has resulted in true growth and an advance in the cause of social justice. The Christian community must look to attempts to secure peace and nonviolence in the human community. With those who work toward the elimination of nuclear arms and all weapons of violence, the Christian must join hands.

That is to say, the Christian community is a group of people which finds itself alongside others in the human enterprise. Wherever there are efforts to do the truth in love freely, and wherever there are efforts to enable the person to become a subject of her or his own history, the Christian is called upon to recognize the traces of grace, and cooperate with it.

It may be useful to note that the two most important efforts with which the Christian community must join hands are those of the women's movement throughout the world and those of persons of developed ecological consciousness. The future of the churches, as well as the future of the human race and the entire cosmos, stands on shaky ground. Our future looks dim unless we can come to learn from those who are envisioning new ways for women and men to collaborate in the human enterprise, and from those who are calling for new ways for human beings to relate to the earth, the environment, and other forms of life.[7]

Uniquely Christian Principles

Principles of natural morality and the efforts to secure peace and justice in the human enterprise are not identical, however, to the vision and principles of a social justice ethic informed and motivated by Christian faith and worship. Christian faith looks to the person as created in the image of God.[8] The human person is viewed as a being endowed with grace who, thereby, participates in the very life of God. Through the exercise of the capacities of knowledge, freedom, and love, he or she lives by grace and more closely manifests the life and presence of God who is truth, freedom, and love. The value and dignity of the person, from the Christian perspective, derive from an understanding of person as image of God who thereby enjoys certain rights. These rights, at their most basic level, assure growth and responsibility so that persons and communities are enabled to do the truth in love freely.

The rights which derive from the value and dignity of the human person created in God's image do not, then, pertain only to securing the growth and development of the person in the physical or material order. Rather, this vision looks to the whole person, especially as regards the God-given capacity for knowledge, freedom, and love, and articulates a Christian ethic in light of this.

In many ways this vision and this ethic are on a higher plane than the principles of a natural morality. Precisely because value and dignity derive from the creative activity of God, a higher vision of the human person is presented in Christianity than in the quest for human justice, pure and simple. A Christian ethic based upon the image of God in the human person requires, then, a different approach to the question of needs and rights than does an approach which focuses upon natural rights and justice.

That having been said, it is nonetheless true that in the pursuit of this higher, Christian ethic, principles of a natural morality cannot be set aside. What is known from the larger human enterprise as regards the nature and dignity of the human person must be respected. For example, the right to a just wage cannot be ignored by Christian establishments on the basis of their pursuit of higher values, or because they operate by religious principles. The same could be said regarding the right to unionize or the right to employment in light of sexual orientation. In the church's own structures and polity, rights which all persons enjoy and which are known by the principles of a natural morality, cannot be set aside or held in abeyance by appeal to a higher ethic. The same needs to be said regarding the ways in which persons are brought before the various courts and judiciary bodies within the Roman Catholic church.[9] The church has done more to respect, protect, and defend human rights than any other body in history. Unfortunately this has been truer in theory than in practice. Human rights, pure and simple, cannot be bypassed, held in abeyance, set aside, or discarded for any reason or principle, especially a religious one.

Eucharist: Paradigm of Communion and Justice

As we have said previously, the sharing of the basic and fundamental elements of bread and wine constitutes an expression of willingness to share at a fundamental and basic level of human existence. Without this willingness to share, no true human justice is possible. To gather together, to break bread and share the cup as an act of remembrance of Jesus Christ, is to stand in solidarity with victims of all ages and of all sorts. An unwillingness to take their side, and indeed to recognize oneself in them, is to defile the bread and the cup, and gives indication of a failure to discern the Lord's Body.

Looking to the Eucharist as paradigm of communion and justice, the Christian community affirms that the reign of God and the Lordship of Jesus Christ are the realities to which all human judgment and action must be submitted. Justice, truth, kindness, peace are the promises of God's reign, when God will be all in all. It is these realities to which the Christian is pledged in the cup and in the crust. Unwillingness to work actively toward the realization of these values is likewise a failure to discern the Lord's Body.

The concern for the social implications of the gospel and the requirements for justice which it places upon those who sit at the Lord's table were abiding concerns for the Apostle Paul. The Christians at Corinth came under his fire precisely because the divisions, quarrels, and refusal to share with those who had less, the poor in their midst, were incompatible with the mystery of Christ's Body celebrated in their eucharistic assembly (1 Cor. 11:17–34). So the problem is not new, but it takes various forms in different historical periods. But the question must be posed time and again: Does our eucharistic sharing express our identity as the Body of Christ, which we have become by grace and Spirit, or is it yet another occasion for discrimination, exercise of domination over the vulnerable and weak, and pious self-absorption?

Quintessential Values of Justice, Peace, and Preference for the Poor

The church is a social body. Like any social body there are values and principles which guide its life. Since the Second Vatican Council there has been greater and greater attention to the fundamental values of justice, peace, and the preferential option for the poor.[10] These values are of such import, that one could say that they are not simply desired in one who calls himself or herself Christian— they are required. That is to say, these values are constitutive of community and of Catholic identity. Again, this is because of the ever-increasing awareness that the kingdom of God was central to the life and ministry of Jesus. At the heart of this "master image" or central symbol are the hallmark values of justice and peace, with a special predilection for the poor—not only the materially poor, but those who are nameless, forgotten, victimized, oppressed, and without hope.

A social body projects its values in ritual. Fourth of July rituals in the United States give occasion to project the values of independence, freedom, self-determination, and so on. Whatever one may care to argue about what is going on in the sacramental life of the church, at a fundamental level there is this process of "value projection." Perhaps as never before, we need to be conscious of the values associated with the kingdom, which we project and promise to live by each time we celebrate sacramentally: justice, peace, and preference for the poor and wounded.

A Christian ethic which derives from word and sacrament looks to those to whom Jesus himself was closest. He kept away from the self-righteous and the proud, the pious and the perfect, and drew near to sinners and those at the edges of society.

Such a Christian ethic, then, accords pride of place to those who are poor and weak, wounded, oppressed, and forgotten. In dealings with others, at the personal, familial, communal, national, and international levels, their place, their dignity, their value must be restored and maintained, above all else. They are looked to as first in the kingdom of God, and a Christian ethic must attempt to shape policy in the socio-political realm so that social structures and political practice may be a more adequate reflection of that reality.

Aside from giving pride of place to the poor and wounded in the attempt to bring about justice, a situation where all may grow, a Christian ethic must look to Jesus' ministry of pardon, forgiveness, reconciliation, and healing, expressed in word and sacrament, as the basis for peace and communion of persons. The communion of persons for which a Christian ethic strives, not based upon principles of natural morality pure and simple, demands the exercise of mercy, forgiveness, and compassion which derive from the power of God in Jesus Christ.

Perhaps this is the clearest example of how a Christian ethic is built upon the principles of natural morality, but calls for a higher integration of those principles within a Christian vision. Many would agree that communion or harmony of persons is a desirable thing. Nations, races, and classes express willingness to secure peace by working for justice. Yet a Christian ethic, which would acknowledge the need for negotiation, toleration, and mutual respect of human rights would also look to the values of mercy, forgiveness, pardon, and reconciliation as necessary keys to lasting peace and harmony.

In our own day, the demands of such an ethic may be seen by looking to the threat of nuclear war. In any discourse about social justice ethics, the possibility of nuclear war cannot be treated as one issue alongside others. The uniqueness of the problem resides in its enormity, its disproportion to other major problems of social ethics. At issue is the absolute destruction of everything as we have ever known it.[11] There are several ethical issues which must be treated in considering nuclear war, and preparation for it. The nuclear arms race is rooted in a hidden idolatry: playing God in our efforts to master and control our destiny through power and might. But the whole arms race belies the fact that we cannot create, or give life, vision, hope, or promise, only that we are fascinated by the capacity to destroy. In the "one-upmanship" between the superpowers one witnesses the erosion of our affiliation with brothers and sisters who, like ourselves, are the fruit of God's parenting. As children of one divine parent, we betray that gift, and erode God's parenting, each time decisions are reached and actions are undertaken to "protect ourselves" through the willed and systematically planned destruction of nations, races, classes, and cosmos. Finally, the nuclear age is also the age of a pathological economy where more than half of our resources are committed to destruction or the threat of destruction.

No one can pretend to offer ready solutions to this problem. Some have attempted to exercise prudent guidance on the issue.[12] Based as it is, however, not simply on the convictions of natural morality, but on the conviction that each and every human being is an *imago Dei*, created in God's image, the fruit of God's parenting, a Christian ethic looks to the realities of mercy, forgiveness, pardon, and reconciliation as the foundation stones for any future, hope, or promise when faced with the possibility of nuclear holocaust.

Faith in Practice

Perhaps the social implications of the gospel are the most difficult to discern and practice. Concern for human rights, peace, justice, and communion of persons demands of contemporary Christians a constant conversion to the message of the gospel and the person of Christ crucified and risen. It requires attention to the morality expressed in the sacraments, especially the Eucharist, and confidence in the grace and Spirit which they offer. But here again, in the area of social justice, decisions are not made for us, and there are no easy answers.

In light of the belief in the value and dignity of the human person, contemporary Christians are called upon to face the many questions which plague our society. Among them, let us single out the issue of work and unemployment.

Human work may be looked at in a variety of ways. It may be viewed in terms of the human person's capacity to produce goods, subdue the earth, and/or serve the needs of the person and community. Whatever position one may care to take on the question of the nature of human work, a Catholic social ethic, informed by the social encyclicals, especially *Mater et Magistra*, *Populorum Progressio*, and *Laborem Exercens*, must reevaluate the nature and function of work in light of the value and dignity of the human person.[13] Work is not simply production for human subsistence. Persons are to be valued over the work they do. Work must contain a certain degree of pleasure, allow for participation and creativity. Hence, in the decisions which face Christians in the world today, especially those First World Christians whose decisions affect millions of others, attention must be given to the need of the human person and community for work which is inclusive of pleasure, participation, and creativity. That is to say, it is not enough to look to work, our own and others', simply in terms of the means whereby we earn our daily bread. It is not simply a question of seeing to it that everyone has a job. It is more a question of building a world within which all may grow, which is the activity of justice, and of recognizing that work, inclusive of the dimensions of pleasure, participation, and creativity, is essential to human dignity and growth.

The practice of the gospel touches upon every dimension of human life, even the most mundane. It is not enough to believe in the dignity and value of human persons. Christians are mandated to decide and act in accord with what is believed. Nothing remains untouched by the vision of Christian faith. Nothing escapes the grasp of God's grace and transforming Spirit.

Making Practical Decisions

The morality expressed in word and sacrament is the horizon in light of which Christians are called upon to make concrete choices when the ethical implications of the gospel demand judgment, decision, and action. Models or methods of decision-making provide us with tools for making choices so that what is believed may be put into practice. Let us look to a few of the models, treated earlier, in order to better understand the way in which concrete choices in the area of social justice might be made.

The values model of decison-making calls upon Christians to articulate those values which are crucial to the message of Jesus, as well as values which are antithetical to the gospel. When faced with a choice involving the building of weapons, the decision would involve choosing between supporting the efforts of those whose aim is to become more powerful through the building of nuclear weapons, or standing under the power of the Spirit alone. Applied to racism, the values model of decision-making enables one to see that the aim in overcoming racism is not the amalgamation of all the races into one. The aim is one of discerning and respecting unique and irreplaceable cultural expressions and a great diversity of communal values.

The discipleship model of decision-making, applied to the problem of discrimination of all sorts, enables one to undertake judgment, decision, and action based on the life of Christ. Hence, as regards the question of discrimination against women in society and in church, what would be the practical consequences in both realms if Christians used this model for decision-making? The ultimate aim of this model is to have no other mind in one than that of Jesus for whom differences between male and female pale in light of the conviction that all are one in him. This is the same one who, after his death, appeared first to the women whose vigilance had not dimmed (Mark 16:1–11; Luke 24:1–11).

The model of interiority enables one to discern those instincts, feelings, and sensibilities which lead us to hold some in respect, while denying respect to others, on the basis of race, class, sex, status, or economic standing.

Faith That Does Justice: In Memory and in Hope

To live in memory of Jesus is to live by a dangerous memory. It is to recognize that the poor and weak hold pride of place, and that the structures and political policies of this world can never be given absolute allegiance. To live by the memory of Jesus Christ is to affirm that forgiveness, pardon, and reconciliation are necessary for true and lasting peace and communion of persons, and to proclaim in liturgy and in life that there is no other way to peace but through the crucified.

To live in memory, the dangerous memory, of Jesus Christ is to recognize that persons and communities must work for justice as the way to peace, while at the same time recognizing the love of God as an absolute in itself. There is no power, other than God's, to which the Christian submits. Ultimately there are no criteria to which the Christian submits judgment, decision, and action other than the Lordship of Jesus Christ and the power of the Spirit.

The ultimate concern of a social justice ethic is to assure the rights, value, and dignity of human persons so that they may become subjects of their own history and thereby enabled to do the truth in love freely in a world where all may grow. Those who work for justice and peace, restoring and maintaining the dignity of the human person, particularly the poor and weak, created in God's own image, become the clearest signs of God's truth, love and freedom in our world, and the most compelling manifestation of the hope and the promise that God's reign is near at hand.

Notes

1. This view poses a false dichotomy. Recent studies in social justice ethics have brought this to the fore. For a brief critique of the false separation of religion and politics see Michael Downey, "Illegal Compassion: The Sanctuary Movement in the United States," *Doctrine and Life* 36, no. 8 (October 1986): 411–19.

2. John Haughey, "Eucharist at Corinth: You Are the Christ," *Above Every Name*, ed. Thomas Clarke (New York: Paulist Press, 1980), pp. 107–33, p. 123.

3. These dualist christological views are ably critiqued, and a useful alternative proposed by Monika Hellwig, "Christology and Attitudes Toward Social Structures," *Above Every Name*, pp. 13–34.

4. See William Dych, "The Dualism in the Faith of the Church," *The Faith that Does Justice*, ed. John Haughey (New York: Paulist Press, 1977), pp. 47–66.

5. David Hollenbach, "A Prophetic Church and the Catholic Sacramental Imagination," *The Faith that Does Justice*, pp. 234–63, p. 254.

6. Brian McDermott, "Power and Parable in Jesus' Ministry," *Above Every Name*, pp. 83–104, p. 84.

7. David Power, "Liturgical Praxis: A New Consciousness at the Eye of Worship," *Worship* 61, no. 4 (July 1987): 290–304, Vice-presidential address delivered at the annual Meeting of the North American Academy of Liturgy, January 1987, Tarrytown, NY.

8. This is one of the central affirmations of the Judeo-Christian tradition. It constitutes the very basis upon which the church's commitment to social justice rests.

9. See Charles E. Curran, *Faithful Dissent* (Kansas City, MO: Sheed & Ward, 1986).

10. This was most clearly articulated at the Second General Meeting of the Latin American Episcopal Council (CELAM) at Medellin, Columbia, 1968, and at the third meeting of CELAM, Puebla, Mexico, 1979. See Gary Mac Eoin and Nivita Riley, *Puebla: A Church Being Born* (New York: Paulist Press, 1980), p. 90ff. This may also be seen in the United States bishops' pastoral on the economy, *Economic Justice for All* (Washington, DC: United States Catholic Conference, 1986).

11. This I have treated at greater length in "Worship Between the Holocausts," *Theology Today* 43, no. 1 (April 1986): 75–87.

12. See the United States Catholic bishops' pastoral letter on war and peace, *The Challenge of Peace: God's Promise and Our Response* (Washington, DC: United States Catholic Conference, 1983).

13. See the United States bishops' pastoral letter on the economy, *Economic Justice for All.*

Select Bibliography

Reference

Documents on the Liturgy, 1963–1979: Conciliar, Papal, and Curial Texts. International Committee on English in the Liturgy. Collegeville, MN: Liturgical Press, 1982.

The Documents of Vatican II. Edited by Walter Abbott, New York: America Press, 1966.

The Rites of the Catholic Church. 2 vols. New York: Pueblo Publishing Co., 1976, 1980.

Liturgy and Sacraments

Austin, Gerard. *Anointing with the Spirit: The Rite of Confirmation.* New York: Pueblo Publishing Co., 1985.

Baptism, Eucharist and Ministry. Faith and Order Commission Paper no. 111. Geneva: World Council of Churches, 1982.

Bausch, William. *A New Look at the Sacraments.* Mystic, CT: Twenty-Third Publications, 1983.

Cooke, Bernard. *Sacraments and Sacramentality.* Mystic, CT: Twenty-Third Publications, 1983.

Dallen, James. *The Reconciling Community: The Rite of Penance.* New York: Pueblo Publishing Co., 1986.

Eigo, Francis A., ed. *The Sacraments: God's Love and Mercy Actualized.* Villanova, PA: Villanova University Press, 1979.

Ganoczy, Alexander. *Becoming Christian: A Theology of Baptism as the Sacrament of Human History.* New York: Paulist Press, 1976.

Gusmer, Charles. *And You Visited Me: Sacramental Ministry to the Sick and Dying.* New York: Pueblo Publishing Co., 1984.

Guzie, Tad. *The Book of Sacramental Basics.* New York: Paulist Press, 1981.

Hellwig, Monika. *The Eucharist and the Hunger of the World.* New York: Paulist Press, 1976.

_____. *The Meaning of the Sacraments.* Dayton, OH: Pflaum Press, 1972.

_____. *Sign of Reconciliation and Conversion.* Wilmington, DE: Michael Glazier, 1982.

Kavanagh, Aidan. *The Shape of Baptism: The Rite of Christian Initiation.* New York: Pueblo Publishing Co., 1978.

Marsh, Thomas. *Gift of Community: Baptism and Confirmation.* Wilmington, DE: Michael Glazier, 1984.

Martos, Joseph. *The Catholic Sacraments.* Wilmington, DE: Michael Glazier, 1983.

_____. *Doors to the Sacred.* Garden City, NY: Doubleday, 1981.

Murray, Donal. *Life and Sacrament: Reflections on the Catholic Vision.* Wilmington, DE: Michael Glazier, 183.

O'Meara, Thomas Franklin. *Theology of Ministry*. New York: Paulist Press, 1983.

O'Neill, Colman. *Sacramental Realism: A General Theory of the Sacraments*. Wilmington, DE: Michael Glazier, 1983.

Power, David N. *Gifts That Differ: Lay Ministries Established and Unestablished*. 2nd ed. New York: Pueblo Publishing Co., 1985.

_____. *Unsearchable Riches: The Symbolic Nature of Liturgy*. New York: Pueblo Publishing Co., 1984.

Schillebeeckx, Edward. *Christ the Sacrament of the Encounter with God*. New York: Sheed & Ward, 1963.

_____. *The Eucharist*. New York: Sheed & Ward, 1968.

_____. *Marriage: Human Reality and Saving Mystery*. New York: Sheed & Ward, 1965.

_____. *The Church with a Human Face: A New and Expanded Theology of Ministry*. New York: Crossroad Publishing Co., 1985.

Seasoltz, R. Kevin, ed. *Living Bread, Saving Cup: Readings on the Eucharist*. Collegeville, MN: Liturgical Press, 1982.

Siegel, Richard, Michael Strassfeld, and Sharon Strassfeld. *The First Jewish Catalog*. Philadelphia: Jewish Publication Society of America, 1973.

Smith, Patricia. *Teaching Sacraments*. Wilmington, DE: Michael Glazier, 1987.

Thomas, David. *Christian Marriage*. Wilmington, DE: Michael Glazier, 1983.

Vaillancourt, Raymond. *Toward a Renewal of Sacramental Theology*. Collegeville, MN: Liturgical Press, 1979.

White, James. *Introduction to Christian Worship*. Nashville: Abingdon Press, 1980.

Willimon, William H. *The Service of God: Christian Work and Worship*. Nashville: Abingdon Press, 1983.

Moral Theology

Cahill, Lisa Sowle. *Between the Sexes*. New York: Paulist Press, 1985.

Clarke, Thomas, ed. *Above Every Name: The Lordship of Christ and Social Systems*. New York: Paulist Press, 1980.

Curran, Charles, and Richard A. McCormick, eds. *Readings in Moral Theology*. 5 vols. to date. New York: Paulist Press, 1979—.

Gula, Richard. *What Are They Saying About Moral Norms?* New York: Paulist Press, 1982.

Gustafson, James M. *Christ and the Moral Life*. Chicago: University of Chicago Press, 1979.

Häring, Bernard. *Free and Faithful in Christ*. 3 vols. New York: Crossroad Publishing Co., 1978–81.

Hanigan, James. *What Are They Saying About Sexual Morality?* New York: Paulist Press, 1982.

Haughey, John C., ed. *The Faith that Does Justice: Examining the Christian Sources for Social Change*. New York: Paulist Press, 1977.

Keane, Philip. *Sexual Morality: A Catholic Perspective.* New York: Paulist Press, 1977.

Kosnik, Anthony, et al. *Human Sexuality: New Directions in American Catholic Thought.* New York: Paulist Press, 1977.

MacNamara, Vincent. *Faith and Ethics.* Washington, DC: Georgetown University Press, 1985.

Niebuhr, H. Richard. *Christ and Culture.* New York: Harper & Row, 1951.

O'Connell, Timothy. *Principles for a Catholic Morality.* New York: Seabury Press, 1978.

Index